Las Vegas *

Little Black Book:

A Guy's Guide to the Perfect Vegas Weekend

Las Vegas

Little Black Book:

A Guy's Guide to the Perfect Vegas Weekend

Las Vegas*
Little Black Book:

A Guy's Guide to the Perfect Vegas Weekend

DAVID deMONTMOLLIN

HIRAM TODD NORMAN

Justin, Charles & Co.
Boston

FIRST U.S. EDITION 2005

ISBN 1-932112-43-X

Library of Congress Cataloging-in-Publication Data is available.

Published in the United States by
Justin, Charles & Co., Publishers, Boston, Massachusetts
www.justincharlesbooks.com

Distributed by National Book Network, Lanham, Maryland
www.nbnbooks.com

10 9 8 7 6 5 4 3 2 1

PRINTED IN THE UNITED STATES OF AMERICA

Contents

Introduction

★..

Your Weekend: You Deserve a Great Time

If you're heading out to Vegas based on the advice of friends or
the lessons learned from a previous trip, you'll probably have a
pretty good time. And why not? A good time is a nearly every-
weekend occurrence; it's watching a game with the guys, heading out for a beer after a long week, winning money from the
guys on the game you're watching, drafting your fantasy football
team. Good times are your bread and butter. *Great* times, on the
other hand, are much harder to come by, but that doesn't mean
you're not deserving of one, especially in Vegas. That's where the
Little Black Book can help, because we know what you want.
You're a guy — one of evolution's simplest creatures, hardwired
from the time of creation (whatever myth you favor) to seek
stimulation from just a few reliable sources: sex, food, strong
drink, and the joyous abandon that can only be achieved by bay-
ing raucously with your friends and a group of secretaries in
from Chicago after you hit your point at the craps table. If you
head out to Sin City armed with the *Little Black Book,* we guarantee you'll have a great time.

Our purpose in writing the *Little Black Book* is to make it easy for
you to create the ultimate guy's weekend, to help you avoid the
traps that will soak up your time and eat up your wallet, and to

ensure you'll leave Las Vegas with a smile on your face and tales to tell for years to come.

This book will provide you with all of the information you need to take the town by the horns and ride it for all it's worth. Every trip can be broken down into a set of key decisions that will make or break your weekend. You need to play things smart, and if you do, good times will follow. You work too hard with too little time off to settle for anything less than getting every ounce of fun out of your much-needed Vegas weekend. Going to Vegas with the guys should be a special event — don't wind up at the departure gate saying, "Next time we'll know to avoid…."

Advice You Can Use

You hear a lot about stories about Las Vegas, some of them true, but unfortunately not many. Come on, who's going to admit how much they lost, how much their hotel room really cost, or how long they had to wait to get into an overcrowded, overpriced nightclub? Maybe the relentless desert heat fries the brain's truth circuits, or maybe they're embarrassed; either way, you're not getting the straight dope.

Enter the *Little Black Book*. It'll help you tune out the static and home in on the right frequency, leading you to great places filled with good times and gorgeous women. Don't expect comprehensive reviews, don't expect any information on family friendly activity, and don't expect advice on romantic destinations. Our sole aim is to provide you, the guy traveling to Sin City for forty-eight hours of hot fun, with a frank, opinionated, insider's guide to chasing up good times for you and the fellas. There are no sucker bets in here, just sure things for good times.

Advice You Can Trust

You don't have much time to spend and you certainly don't have cash to waste chasing mirages in the desert, so why trust the

Little Black Book? You can trust this book because the guys behind it know whereof they speak. David deMontmollin has lived the Vegas life most guys can only dream about. Not to brag, but it's true.

As chronicled on the Travel Channel's reality TV show, *American Casino*, David spends his days in casino marketing and his nights out on the town. Every other book about Las Vegas is written by a travel writer who blows into town and writes reviews. These people may be fine travel writers, but they lack the perspective of a Vegas insider. On the other hand, most insiders don't go out to the Strip when they're not working, and in fact they do everything possible to avoid guys like you. That's where David begs to differ.

While Las Vegas might be America's adult playground, it's David's backyard. While many come to Vegas to hang out on the Strip, he lives there (literally), spending his nights on the other side of the velvet rope. Every weekend David takes charge of a pack of guys in town visiting. Usually they're friends or friends of friends looking for a good time, and David delivers. He sets them up with the Vegas weekend they've dreamt about.

You've found the guy who plays in the Vegas big leagues, and he wants you to have as good a time as he does.

How to Use this Book

This book is intended to help you during the three phases of your trip: planning, executing and remembering.

Dreaming Las Vegas — Planning Out Your Trip

You need to figure out way in advance of your arrival where you're going to stay and how you're going to spend your nights out on the town. There are also many daytime activities that you'll need to plan in advance. Figure out ahead of time what will make for a memorable trip, get buy-in from the boys, and book some reservations now.

Viva Las Vegas — Executing the Details
Once you're on the ground you'll need to get the lay of the land: Put the *Little Black Book* in your back pocket and hit the town. We'll tell you where to spend your time and money every step of the way. Want to meet women? This is Vegas, baby! That's what the *Little Black Book*'s all about.

Leaving Las Vegas — Remembering Your Trip
Many a traveler has commented on the unreality of Vegas. It's like another planet, and before you leave you have to step into the air lock and decompress. When you do leave, you need to be armed with stories for the nine-to-fivers back home. Your experience in Vegas needs to be top-notch, loaded with memories that will last you a lifetime. The *Little Black Book* will show you how to create memorable experiences, and how to tell about them afterward.

The Appendices: Quick References
The appendices in the back of the book are reference guides that summarize the information in the book. The first appendix contains six different hour-by-hour itineraries to use for planning your own trip. The second appendix contains reference lists of places outlined in the book to make arrangements and book reservations.

Get to Work/Have Fun
You need to decide right now to take ownership of your trip — don't let it "just happen" or you'll wind up broke, bitter and disappointed. Read on, make plans, have fun.

PART I

Dreaming Las Vegas

Chapter 1

24 Hours in Sin City

★ ....

Waking up in the morning, he opens the curtains that keep the bright desert sun out of his tenth-floor apartment. He never fails to be amazed by what he sees. The epicenter of fun in the modern world opens up beneath his window: the Las Vegas Strip. Energy just breathes from it, like waves of heat off the desert. He stares out, but his eyes can never completely focus because there is so much to take in. It's a view that you never really get used to. Just the sight is enough to get lost in, the row after row of casinos stretching as far as the eye can see, each one more remarkable than the one before.

Eventually, he realizes that he has been standing there for a while. He takes a last sip of his morning joe and takes a deep breath. It all seems so peaceful from this vantage point. He knows that the first step out of his door signals another day in America's adult paradise.

Walking out of the Jockey Club in his hand-tailored, pin-striped suit and newly polished shoes, he breathes in the crisp desert air. The sun is already out and a warm breeze is blowing. He puts the top down on the midnight blue Chrysler Prowler, turns the key, and lets the engine purr. Pulling out of the parking lot onto the Strip, he knows that his is not the average working guy's typical morning commute.

At this time of day the Las Vegas Strip is a ghost town. Tens of thousands of part-time partyers are out of sight, out of mind, sleeping off another long night. Reminiscing about the night before, he knows it will be hard to top it, but for him Vegas just keeps getting better.

He can't really call his day at the office, work. His career as a young casino executive in one of the top resorts in town is his whole life. He lives and breathes casinos. He is a casino freak. From the moment he walked into his first casino, he knew he wanted to dedicate his life to it. This is his business, and he knows that he can never go back to a normal job.

He pushes the envelope on what is considered a normal workday. Today he is running three events at once: an audition for go-go dancers for the next big concert, a promotional bikini calendar photo shoot, and a high stakes casino blackjack tournament. Switching back and fourth between the simultaneous events, it is amazing how he is always in control and maintains his cool.

Casinos are a 24-hour business, so he is a 24-hour guy. The cell phone could ring at any time. Whether it's a player issue, or a bachelor party, he's always available.

A friend from Philadelphia is calling him. Today, he's setting up a guys' weekend for a bachelor party. He has it all set. The bachelor parties that he throws are legendary. Every arrangement and detail is taken care of. Limos, dinners, private pool cabanas; ironically, in a city with so much to choose from, he leaves no detail to chance. He has set these parties up a hundred times, and by now he knows perfection.

Networking is crucial in this town. Leaving the casino at the end of the day, he heads out to a cocktail party at one of the top restaurants in town. Working the room and dishing out business cards, he knows that in Vegas knowing the right people is everything. At the bar, he orders a gin martini, straight up with olives. Old-school.

He enjoys the vintage Vegas, and strives to keep the Vegas traditions alive. A king-cut prime rib for dinner, a good cigar with a shot of Sambuca, lounge singers doing classic Sinatra, stage shows with topless showgirls, Elvis impersonators, and magicians are some of the things he loves about this place.

He knows where to go every night. The Strip is his backyard, his playground. Buzzing around it, he takes the routes known to only the most experienced taxi drivers in this town. Everyone else is stuck in traffic while he pulls up to the back-of-casino valets.

Time to stop off and meet some friends of a friend from Chicago for a quick drink, and to give them a little Vegas 101. He's early, sees a cute girl at the end of the bar, buys her a drink and checks his watch. Out of the corner of his eye he can't help but notice a pack of guys wandering aimlessly through the hotel lobby. They're in a state of shock. There are just too many things to do in this town, and their lack of direction seems to have gotten the better of them. He can't help but scribble an evening itinerary onto a cocktail napkin and pass if off to them. If they follow his advice, they'll have an amazing night. After a quick drink with the guys and a phone number from his new lady friend, it's off to bed.

He takes a quick shower and stands in his robe gazing out the window. The Bellagio's fountains are starting again. The water is dancing to the music while the rest of the Strip glows brightly behind. It's hard to get over it, the most beautiful sight he has even seen, even though he has seen it a thousand times.

After a few hours of sleep it's time to start all over again. For most guys it's a dream come true, for him it's just another day in Sin City.

* * * *

This is a day in David deMontmollin's life in Las Vegas, twenty-four hours of doing what he loves in a place he loves. Now, it's his mission to show you how to make the most of your time here. He knows he's not the only one who loves Las Vegas: Last year alone more than 35,000,000 people visited Sin City. It's one of the top tourist destinations in the United States, and it's *the* top destination for what has become a staple of the Vegas Strip: the guy's weekend/bachelor party weekend.

Every weekend of every month of the year, hundreds of thousands of men come to Las Vegas. Who are they, and what are they looking for?

They are men, single or married, twenty-one or over (if you're not twenty-one, put this book aside for a few years, guy, until you're old enough to play the games and drink at the bar) who come for business or pleasure. Of course, in Las Vegas, business *is* pleasure; the Las Vegas Convention Center is booked virtually every week of the year with tens of thousands of businesspeople looking to mix work and play.

Increasingly, they are groups of guys who come specifically to drink and gamble, to meet women or even just to look at them (Vegas is the strip club capital of the world), to eat well, stay up all night, smoke good cigars, and relax in the company of their friends. Maybe they're here to send a friend off to the land of married nine-to-fivers in high style.

They are, in a word, YOU, and if you're holding this book, it means you're smart and motivated enough to want to not just visit Las Vegas but to fully experience the incredible smorgasbord of diverse pleasures this town has to offer.

Well, we've got your back. Welcome to the world of the *Las Vegas Little Black Book*.

Chapter 2

Busting the Vegas Myth

★...

Las Vegas is a city that inspires legends. The stories we all hear about Sin City make it out to be a combination of Amsterdam and Al Capone's Chicago. Women. 24-hour cocktail lounges. Celebrities. An endless river of cash flowing right before your eyes. You can roll into town in your old Ford, bet your paycheck, get comped the penthouse suite, and go home in a chartered jet. There are a million stories in the naked city, and Vegas is more naked than most. Everything you've heard is actually true — or at least maybe it was once, for some other guy. Today, the man visiting Las Vegas for an all-out weekend needs to learn the facts about some of the classic Vegas myths before he gets off of the plane and spends his whole trip chasing a mirage. One thing is certain: Las Vegas thrives on its own mythology. The town knows what people want, and does very little to demystify itself. In order to ensure that you'll get the most out of your Vegas trip — whether for a night, a weekend, or longer — you'll need to clear your head of some of the most pervasive, pernicious rumors and illusions. Then you can start to enjoy the reality of this ultimate destination for fun-loving guys.

To understand the origins of the Vegas myth, you need to take a look at the history of the city itself. Las Vegas has become the party center of the universe, but it didn't start out that way.

Old Vegas

Las Vegas boomed with the building of the Hoover Dam. In the 1930s, thousands of workers spent years building the dam, and they needed something to do with their free time. Gambling was small-time then, just a couple of craps tables in some rundown bars. But still, people began traveling here, mostly from Los Angeles, to gamble.

The proliferation of gaming boomed with the creation of resorts, most famously the Flamingo, built by L.A. gangster Benjamin "Bugsy" Siegel. Las Vegas suddenly became a travel destination, a fact not lost on some of the "families" in New York and Chicago. In addition to classing up this desert town, the Flamingo signaled the beginning of the presence of serious mob money in developing little old Las Vegas.

The Rat Pack Days and the Advent of Comps

As the profits from casinos lined the mob bosses' pockets, there was increased competition for gambling dollars. Enter, in the 1950s, some guys named Frank Sinatra, Sammy Davis, Jr., and Dean Martin. These Vegas legends (you can still see them in one of the Rat Pack tribute revues) helped turn Las Vegas into a tourist destination. With big-name talent, good food, and nice hotels, what used to be a day trip to a desert town became a vacation stay. As the town took off, the casinos began to compete with one another to attract and hang on to as many players as they could get. So began the age of the comp. Comping (for complimentary) is the practice of giving away freebies to gamblers: free hotel rooms, steak dinners, nightclub passes, drinks, bottles of booze or champagne. Properties were famous for doing just about anything to retain loyal players; comps were thrown around like nobody's business. Today, if a first-time visitor knows only one thing about Las Vegas, it's that he can expect to get stuff for free. Or so he thinks.

Howard Hughes and the Big Corporations

Howard Hughes saw opportunity in the desert and began buying up the Strip. He invested capital into the casinos to make them bigger and better than before. The mob dollars could only go so far without attracting too much unwanted attention. Once the unions fell under investigation for their investments into Sin City, the mafia guys had no ability to maintain an even semi-legitimate presence in Vegas. So, they packed up and moved back East. Publicly held corporations began to buy up Vegas as an exploitable cash cow.

The 1990s Boom and the Advent of the Mega Resorts

In 1989, developer Steve Wynn opened the Mirage, and Las Vegas embarked on a boom of mega resort casinos. The Mirage was followed by Treasure Island, Luxor, Excalibur, New York-New York, MGM Grand, Mandalay Bay, Paris, Venetian, and the Aladdin. As room inventory increased, so did the need to fill them. The Strip properties discounted their rooms heavily to get players. Any loss a hotel incurred could be balanced out with casino profits.

Players wised up. They worked the casino comp systems to play just enough to get everything they wanted. How-to books clued everyone in on just how to get what you want from the casino without losing your shirt.

Technology Takes Hold: Electronic Player Tracking Systems

Casinos developed player tracking systems: a computer database that tracks each player's amount bet, won, and lost. The tracking systems allow casino management to analyze each player on an individual basis and reward him or her accordingly. Gone are the days of the pit boss's discretion in handing out comps. Today, the casino can determine the profitability of each player, so that he or she can be comped to a precise level, and so that no one will get rewards that aren't earned by putting money in play.

The Modern Day Vegas: Mega Mergers Means Less Competition

A few years ago the many mega properties of the Strip waged war for a select group of high rollers and hard-core players. Today, that's all changed. Although every property has its own targets for increased year-over-year profits, the rules have changed because most of them are on the same team. Now only a small handful of publicly traded corporations control the Strip. The result is less competition and less incentive to keep a player's business, knowing as they do that the only competition is another property that's part of the same company. Reduced competition for players means fewer freebies. As we'll see, the days of the comp (with some exceptions) are over.

10 LAS VEGAS MYTHS

✶ Vegas Myth #1: Comps: Everyone Gets 'Em ✶

Without question, the number one myth about Las Vegas is that a regular guy can get — and should get, and will get — something for nothing. If you gamble, be prepared to receive comped rooms, shows, limos, and fine dining.

The Truth

If you've got visions of complimentary accommodations and hobnobbing with Bruce Willis in the VIP room at Body English in your head, either take out a home equity loan or leave those dreams at home.

You know that classic line that all of the casinos in Vegas were built on the losses of suckers? Well, it's true. As with most things in life, in Vegas there's no such thing as a free lunch, or even a free cocktail. Everything costs. No casino is going to give you something substantial for free. They might give you a little something as an enticement to get your play, but you have to play real money to get real rewards. What you're given is measured out in an elaborate comp system.

So, what can you expect the casinos to give you on this trip? Well, you might get a coupon book, or perhaps a hat or shirt, when you sign up for the rewards club. Aside from that, expect to get free drinks while you play. Not quite as glamorous as the chartered jets and limos that some players get, but that shouldn't prevent you from having a good time. You won't get much for free, but that doesn't mean you should spend everything you have just to try to get tickets to a show. If you want tickets to a show, save yourself the headaches and just buy them.

✴ Vegas Myth #2: Hotel Rooms are Cheap ✴

Since casinos make so much money on the casino floor, they give away rooms for cheap to get people to stay there. Only suckers pay more than $99 a night.

The Truth

Times have changed. While Vegas casino hotels are probably still, on average, the least expensive of many resort destinations, that all changes on popular weekends. The number and frequency of big weekends in Vegas seems to grow every year, and now includes the Super Bowl, March Madness, NASCAR, New Year's, St. Patrick's Day, and the rodeo. At those times and many others, room rates can get pretty steep (that's right, you might have to pay an arm and a leg because the rodeo is in town). Truth be told, there's always something big going on in Vegas. From boxing events to big concerts to mega conventions, each weekend in Las Vegas there is something going on that drives up room rates. For a basic room at one of the better Strip properties you should expect to spend $200 to $300 a night — still better than Manhattan rates, but the gap is closing.

✳ Vegas Myth #3: Dining: The $5 Buffet ✳

If you're hungry you can always get great food for next to no money at a Vegas buffet.

The Truth

The days of the cheap buffets are over. Hotels used to lure in tourists with inexpensive food in the hope that they would lose big in the casino. Now casinos are more sophisticated about the players they try to attract, so they quit operating food and beverage at a loss. There are still a couple of bargains out there, but they are usually at the third-tier casinos that are fighting for survival.

In addition, casinos have an image to maintain. Low prices give the impression of low quality. Would you eat a $1.99 prime rib? You'd probably think that it's so thin you could see through it and the meat is not fit for human consumption (and you'd be right). By setting higher prices in the food and beverage outlets, they attract people with money. Casinos want to maintain their overall image and attract the type of players who will spend lots of money, not just nurse a free beer at the nickel slots.

✳ Vegas Myth #4: Girls: They're Everywhere and Easy to Meet ✳

Girls, girls, girls. They are everywhere in Vegas and they are in the mood to party. They're out to have fun, so everyone should be able to score every night.

The Truth

Yes, there are girls in Vegas. There are thousands of them on any given day, and they *are* in the mood to party. But, you have to know where to find them. You can't just wander the Strip hoping to bump into them.

When you do find them, you need to be as creative, stylish, and resourceful as you would be back home if you want to meet and hang out with them. In fact, you must be more so. Single women in Vegas are looking for adventure; they need to tell Vegas stories when they get home, just like you do, but while there are tens of thousands of women in town, there are tens of thousands of men, too. While you're here you've got a lot more competition. Come on like a mope and you won't stand a chance.

✴ Vegas Myth #5: Getting Around. It's Easy to Get There from Here ✴

Casino hotels are right next to each other. It's easy to get from one property to another. You can always walk or just jump in a cab.

The Truth

You have to remember these are the largest hotels in the world, and just getting from one end of the hotel to the other is difficult. Casinos like Mandalay Bay and MGM Grand are massive complexes. You'll need to give yourself time when you want to get from one property to the next. If your friend is staying at the property next door, plan to spend a half hour just getting there.

Some properties, while technically on the Strip, are set way back from the street, so even when you make it out of the front door you still have to hike it to make to the Strip. Bally's and Caesars, for example, are a good five-minute walk just to make it from the front door to the sidewalk.

There are thousands of taxis in Vegas, but they can only pick up at specified hotel entrances; they are not allowed to pick fares up on the Strip. So, if you decide to walk it, and change your mind once you're halfway down the sidewalk and it's high noon and 100 degrees, you'll need to walk all the way to the taxi stand at the next property to catch a cab. On the weekends, expect the cab line to be long enough for you to sober up.

✴ Vegas Myth #6: Hotels: You Just Need a Room, ✴ It Doesn't Matter Where

You are going to be partying so hard in Vegas that you'll never be in your room, so it doesn't matter where you are going to stay. Besides, you can play at any hotel you want — you don't need to be staying there.

The Truth
Your hotel is your headquarters for fun. It is the place you will spend the majority of your time, if only because you have to start and finish your day there. In reality, most guys will spend more time at the hotel than they may think. You will eat many meals there out of convenience, and the casino center bar will serve as your meeting place for your group. Face it, your hotel is the heartbeat of your weekend in Vegas. Don't cheap out.

Hotels in Las Vegas vary greatly. Do a little research to make sure the one you choose is full of the people you want to party with. You won't enjoy Bellagio if your group of guys is more in tune with the Hard Rock Hotel.

And, while you can play wherever you like, many of the property amenities are for guests only, and they get preferential treatment. For example, the pool is a place that is off-limits to non-guests, so don't even try to sneak your way in. Make sure the place you stay gives you lots of options.

✴ Vegas Myth #7: Strip Clubs: All Strip Clubs Are Created Equal ✴

You have been to strip clubs back home. You know what they are like. Vegas clubs are no different.

The Truth
Las Vegas is the strip club capital of the world, and they blow away the clubs that you are used to. Girls fly here from all over the country just to dance on the busy weekends. The rules are

different here because of the number of clubs, the party atmosphere, and the river of cash flowing freely.

Just like the hotels, the strip clubs vary. Not every one is right for you. Each club targets a different crowd. Choose ahead so you don't wind up at a place that doesn't serve alcohol and has a cover charge that's triple what you're willing to pay. Just like anything else in Vegas, if you don't to your homework, you'll get burned.

✶ Vegas Myth #8: Party Town: Everyone Is Here to Have Fun ✶

When you think of Vegas, you think of a crazy party: hot women dancing half-naked out of limo moonroofs, Elvis impersonators on every corner, and go-go dancers at every bar. The champagne flows like water, and everyone you meet is on their own wild adventure, because this is Vegas, baby!

The Truth

Here is a little known fact: the age of the average visitor to Las Vegas is fifty. Five-0. As much as you might want it to be, this whole town is not built for the young, beautiful party crowd. It's built for people to spend money. So, you need to choose the right places to find your kind of people or you'll spend most of the time wandering around looking for action.

Not all accommodations, dining, and entertainment are made for the partying bunch. If you stay at the wrong place you'll probably come face-to-face with a hotel full of conventioneers in town for a trade show who aren't thrilled with the prospect of a pack of rowdy drunk guys keeping them up all night.

Also, the reality is that Vegas wears people out over time. The first day you might be downing shots, staying up all night, and pounding cans of Redbull. By day two you are still going, but have lost a step. By the third day, your body is exhausted, your spirit is wasted, your mind is mush, and you're just wishing it would all be over soon. You need to pace yourself to stay in the race.

✶ Vegas Myth #9: 24-Hour Town: Nothing Closes in Vegas ✶

24 hours a day, 7 days a week, 365 days a year, Vegas goes off. You can always find something to do.

The Truth

Yes, the casinos are open 24 hours. Yes, the bars are open 24 hours. Yes, you can dine for 24 hours. But no, not everyone is doing that. And do you really want to? The truth is that 4 a.m. in Las Vegas can feel like you've wandered onto the set of a zombie movie. The heady, buzzy casino vibe changes in the early morning hours; the bars empty, the diners are quiet and pensive. You can have a great time on an all-nighter, but you've got to plan it out or you might find that the hot spot you wanted to hit shut down hours before you're willing to call it quits. Sometimes it's better to rest up and save your energy for the premium party rather than search for that elusive early morning good time.

✶ Vegas Myth #10: The Desert. Vegas is always hot. ✶

When you think of Vegas weather, you think hot, dry desert air. There is no water here, so it must be hot all the time.

The Truth

It gets cold in Vegas. Though it is in the desert, its latitude is about equal to Atlanta's. This is not the tropics. The pools close November through March, and October and April it can be pretty brisk and windy. Check the forecast before you pack.

In the desert, when the sun isn't shining, the temperature can drop dramatically. It might be 80 degrees during the day but 50 at night. Don't get stuck in shorts and a T-shirt at sundown. Prepare for the elements and pack smart.

Let's Get Started

Now that the *Little Black Book* has busted some of the popular myths about Vegas, you still want to go, right? Sure you do. Look at it this way: By any reasonable standard, Las Vegas shouldn't even exist. It's an anomaly. It's an oasis in the desert, a cathedral of pleasure where time, money, and workaday worries have no meaning. There's a lot of fun to be had in this town; it just helps to walk in with your eyes open. There are plenty of costly mistakes to be made; we just want to help you avoid as many of them as possible.

Chapter 3

Rally Your Troops:
Take Charge of Your Trip

★···

We've seen way too many trips that start like this: You're at the office on a Friday afternoon, rushing to meet some end-of-the-quarter numbers, when you look at your watch and realize you need to head out to the airport in fifteen minutes. You only had time to throw some toiletries and semi-clean, wrinkled clothes into a carry-on before you dashed to work this morning. But hey, you take solace in the fact that *you're going to Vegas*, and you'll be out all night, anyway; it's not like you need more than one change of clothes. You plan to pick up one of your buddies on the way to the airport. Your other friends will meet you in Sin City tonight. They're coming in from all over, at all sorts of times, but it doesn't matter because they know you can be found in the casino at the hotel.

There's no need to sit around in your hotel room or at the airport waiting for them; they're adults and you have some gaming to do. Your travel pal is going to hit the bar while you gamble; it's been a rough week, and he's looking to tie one on, and perhaps pick up a cocktail waitress or two.

Fast-forward to tomorrow morning: You and your buddy are lying in bed passed out. One of your friends was delayed, so he's arriving in two hours; another's just getting in, and no one's heard from the last guy (he spent twenty minutes pounding on your door, but you were too wasted to hear, so he went back to the casino bar). We can safely bet that the last thing your merry group wants to do is wait around for four or five hours until your dead-broke, hung-over, sorry selves can sober up and let them into the room. Boy, this is the start of a great trip! Unfortunately, what you don't realize now is that when your whole troop finally assembles, that's when the real problems will start.

It turns out that one of the guys wants to hit a strip joint this afternoon and the casinos tonight. Two of the others are interested in checking out "Old-school Vegas" downtown, and you want to watch a couple of games at a sportsbook. Looks like your guys' weekend is kind of falling apart, and it is only day one. As Saturday becomes Sunday, you can't really seem to get on the same page with your pals and, aside from a breakfast, you don't really see much of them until it's time to go home.

What happened? This was going to be such a great time but it went by so fast that you never even really got to hang out together, which (aside from the booze, women, and gambling) was the whole point of the trip. Well, face it: No one took any ownership of your trip to begin with. Everyone was so busy that they never really had time to think about the trip before they arrived, and the group's "it's Vegas, it's not really hard to have a good time here" attitude made what could have been a great time into pretty good, very expensive time. Let this be a cautionary tale: Do your part to make sure your whole crew has a great time in Vegas.

Think Ahead: How to Prevent Your Trip from Going Down in Flames

By following just a few simple rules, adopting some guidelines, doing some research, delegating some duties, and taking formal responsibility, you can rule the world as the Vegas-savvy man-god that you are. Or at least you'll have a much, much better guys' trip to Sin City.

Take Ownership

One of the biggest mistakes that most guys make when they plan a trip to Vegas is that no one is willing to take charge. Who wants to be the hard-ass guy issuing orders and handing out agendas? After all, this isn't some sales meeting of mid level software execs back in Fresno, this is Vegas! You left all that behind, so chill, book a flight and a room, and make the rest up as you go along. Right? Wrong! Don't spend your whole trip to Vegas improvising; you'll wind up wasting a lot of time and money. Somebody's got to step up, take charge, and get it done. You're playing in the major leagues here: Do your line-up card ahead of game time or get ready to have a bench full of pissed-off bonus babies on your hands. No one is saying you should become General Patton barking out orders to your troops, but you *should* become a project manager. Don't count on one of your friends to step up to the plate and figure some of this stuff out — do it yourself. Grow a pair and put together a game plan. You're the one who was smart enough to pick up this book, so you should be the one to call a few of the shots. Here's how.

Plan Your Play – Play Your Plan

Now that you've admitted somebody's got to be Head Boy and it might as well be you, the first things you've got to decide are the big-ticket items. What are the milestone, watershed experiences you and your group will share that will make this trip the stuff of office water cooler legend? A couple of tips:

♠ Don't let this decision slide till you're on the ground. You'll discover plenty of serendipitous little thrills in Vegas, but those are the details, not the tent pole experiences.

❧ Don't overbook yourself. A guy's weekend goes by awfully fast: In thirty-six to forty-eight hours you'll be on the plane back home. There's only time for, say, four or five major life-altering experiences. It ought to be enough.

For convenience' sake we've organized the *Little Black Book* into simple categories for your use and amusement. Here are the primary elements you need to integrate into your trip plan:

1. Travel – Travel smart, cheap, and together.

2. Accommodations – Stay at a place that meets the needs of your group.

3. Dining – Make smart dining choices that leave the group satisfied.

4. Daytime Entertainment – Don't sleep all day; there is plenty to do during the sunlight hours.

5. Gaming – Gamble the right games at the right time without going broke.

6. Nighttime Entertainment – Don't stand in line for hours; find places that will keep your group partying hard.

7. Gentlemen's Clubs – Learn the lay of the land and how to have fun without being intimidated.

In subsequent chapters the *Little Black Book* will help you determine the best fit for all of these things. While all of these should be considered, don't assume that you'll be able to get consensus on every single aspect of your vacation — and that's fine. Choose your battles in advance and make those the tent poles of your good time.

𝖸 Classic Vegas Mistake

Inviting the Downer: Don't let the wrong guy onto the guest list. If you have a friend who is selfish, obnoxious, depressing, or downright annoying, leave him at home. One time, a group of friends came out to Las Vegas and were all having a great time when one of them decided he wanted a break. He told everyone he was going watch a movie, and he never returned. The group went back to the hotel, convinced a bellhop to let them into his room and discovered their friend's bags were gone. The whole group flipped out and spent most of the day trying to figure out what had happened. Had he gotten sick suddenly? Had his girlfriend back home been in a car crash? Had he fallen on his head, suffered amnesia, and was even now wandering the Strip in a daze? Calls and e-mails went unreturned. Finally, the "friend" called a day later to say that he had just decided to fly home. This group wasted a day on a flake who never should have been on the guest list to start with.

Sample Itinerary

Friday:

8:00 p.m. – Dave, Alan, Miguel, Scott, and Trey arrive in Las Vegas.

8:30 p.m. – Limo to Treasure Island. Dave, Alan, and Miguel check into a suite; Scott and Trey are in an adjoining room. Freshen up and have first celebratory drink in the suite.

9:30 p.m. – Quick bite to eat at the snack shop. Need fuel to carry through the night.

10:00 p.m. – Drinks at the center bar. Establish the lay of the land.

11:00 p.m. – Hit Kaunaville for dueling pianos and cheesy Vegas fun. Buy girls some shots and see where it goes from there.

1:00 a.m. – Play some craps now that the crowd at the tables has died off.

2:00 a.m. – Late night snack at the coffee shop.

3:00 a.m. – Sleep.

Saturday:

11:00 a.m. – Brunch at the pool café. Read the sports section and make some bets on the afternoon basketball games.

1:00 p.m. – Hit the Big Shot at the Stratosphere.

3:00 p.m. – The Strip "Daiquiri Dash". Going from one daiquiri bar to another and seeing what goes on. Try to find some female companionship for later tonight.

5:30 p.m. – Shower and change clothes.

6:30 p.m. – Meet up at the center bar for some drinks.

7:00 p.m. – Rent limo for the night. Cruise the Strip and look for ladies to join in on the fun.

8:30 p.m. – Steak house dinner. Martinis, rib eyes and red wine.

10:00 p.m. – Smoke a cigar and have an after dinner drink.

11:00 p.m. – Limo to Treasures gentlemen's club. Drinks and dances with the ladies.

3:00 a.m. – Taxi back to Treasure Island for some late night pai gow poker.

4:00 a.m. – Sleep

Sunday:
10:00 a.m. – Room service delivers coffee and omelets to room

12:00 p.m. – Check out of room

12:30 p.m. – Make some bets on football games, relax at the sportsbook.

2:00 p.m. – Massage, steam, sauna and shower in the Rock Spa.

4:00 p.m. – Taxi to airport

6:00 p.m. – Depart

The Upside to Taking Ownership:

You might be asking yourself "why me?" The better question is, "why *not* you?" Okay, that was lame, but at the risk of sounding like Tony Robbins, it's true. If you are the one doing the planning and legwork for this trip:

- ✺ you'll get to ensure that you're going to have time to do the things that you want to in Sin City. Project-managing the trip is not a completely selfless act.

- ✺ you'll be the hero. By providing direction for your easily confused brethren, you will be rewarded with drinks, toasts, and maybe a free lap dance courtesy of your suddenly impressed friends.

🍸 Classic Vegas Mistake

Inviting the Spoiler: We had a friend of a friend join us on a jaunt to Vegas only to have him ruin everyone's trip. He was a "Vegas regular" who had made far more money than the rest of the guys on the trip. He set about to change long-standing reservations and get expensive bottle service because he "knew how to have fun in Vegas." He was getting bottles of liquor sent up to the room that could easily have been purchased just outside the hotel for one-tenth the price. He threw the whole group off, and they wound up spending far more money than they were planning to, simply because they let him highjack the trip. True Story.

←→ LAS VEGAS, LAND OF DISTRACTION

There's an old saying in the sales game, "if you can't convince them, confuse them," and no place on earth is this truer than in Las Vegas. From the moment you land, there are signs throughout the airport trying to tell you where to go and what to do. Once you get in your cab there are little booklets filled with places that are "voted best in Las Vegas." When you check into your room you'll find at least one magazine loaded with shows, sights, and restaurants to check out. Step into the casino of your hotel and you'll be bombarded with a flood of flashing lights and confusing sounds. Everyone wants your time and money. Without a game plan, you're playing a losing hand.

Have you noticed?

1. The Floors:

The carpet that they use on casino floors isn't anything you're going to be able to get installed from Carpet World. All of the flooring is an assortment of busy patterns and bizarre color schemes. This is no accident: The floors are designed to make you subconsciously avoid looking at them. You're not going to play a table game if you don't see it, so the casino wants your attention focused at eye level.

2. The Ceilings:

While there are lovely sky-painted ceilings and frescoes high above the Grand Canal Shoppes at the Venetian, they are noticeably absent in the casino. All of the action takes place at, or just above, head level. Rarely is there anything in the casino that you need to look up at to see. Again, they want your attention at eye level.

3. Geographical Points of Reference:

There are no landmarks in a casino. No compasses to get your bearings. You can't see the exits. If it weren't for cocktail waitresses circulating like miniskirted angels of mercy, a lonely traveler could die of thirst. The large statues that decorate the Forum Shops at Caesars are nowhere to be found in the casino. You can't tell one row of slots from the next, and the next. As you get back into the casino you'll be hard-pressed to be able to pick out a place to meet. You can't say "meet me at the blackjack tables"; they're everywhere.

4. Straight Lines:

Straight lines aren't just lacking on the carpet, they're lacking everywhere. It's impossible to walk in a straight line from one end of the casino floor to the other. You will inevitably find a couple of table games in your path, or a row of slots inexplicably placed in the center of what seemed to be a clear route across the floor. In case you were immune to visual distraction, why not just place a physical barrier in your way.

> ### ⅋ Classic Vegas Mistake
>
> **Singled Out:** Las Vegas has perfected the art of the gratuity. There's plenty of grease being served up here, and it's not just at the buffets. Don't wind up high and dry when it's time to tip. You'll be handing out dollar bills like crazy in Sin City, so make sure you have at least $10 in singles with you when you board the plane. You'll need to tip the cab ($3) or limo driver ($5), and the bellhop ($2 per bag) before you even get to your room. Asking a bellhop for change from a twenty so you can tip him $2 makes you feel low, so make sure you're packing some singles in that bankroll to green up some palms.

💰 GETTING READY TO ROLL

Get prepared for your trip. This involves not only packing the right things, but also getting in the Vegas spirit and honing your gambling skills.

You should pack light. No one wants to have to wait at the baggage carousel after arriving, and you certainly don't want to suffer the baggage check line at the end of your trip. Stick with the essentials and you'll be fine.

5 Things to Bring

1. <u>Slacks and a Dress Shirt</u>: Show some class. Remember: A few places have dress codes, and so do some women.

2. <u>Black Dress Shoes with Rubber Soles</u>: You really only need one pair of shoes while in Vegas. Choose a shoe that is comfortable to walk in during the day, but will be dressy enough to wear at night.

3. <u>A Sport Jacket</u>: It gets cold at night in Vegas. You need a light sports jacket for walks from one casino to another while maintaining a level of class. You can also wear a nice, heavy, solid color pullover.

4. <u>Febreze</u>: It's smoky in Vegas. A few shots of this will get a second or third wear out of any garment. You should probably douse your dirty clothes pile, too, so it doesn't stink up your room.

5. <u>Bankroll</u>: Bring as much as you can, but not so much that the old lady throws you out of the house, or your fiancée breaks off the engagement because you blew the money earmarked for your wedding DJ.

5 Things to Leave Behind

1. <u>A Second Jacket</u>: One is enough; dowse yours with Febreze the next morning and you'll be ready to roll.

2. <u>Sports Jerseys</u>: Save them for your Super Bowl party. If you must, and we mean must, wear one, only do it during the day and don't carry around this book. We have an image to maintain.

3. <u>Sweatpants</u>: This isn't the local tavern or your living room, this is Vegas; show a little respect.

4. <u>Baseball Hat</u>: Okay, these are acceptable during the day (especially if you're balding and the only other alternative is a burned scalp) but if you wear one at night you will see no action. None.

5. <u>Your Cares</u>: If you even think about work, your car payment, your annoying neighbor, or how you're going to pay for this trip, once you get on the plane be prepared for one of your friends to smack you.

3 Ways to Practice Gambling

1. <u>Study Up:</u> Go to a gambling Web site and study up on the basics of blackjack, craps and pai gow poker. You don't need to study the games you are not going to play, so unless you've got a serious James Bond fixation, forget about baccarat.

2. <u>Avoid the Systems:</u> Don't get caught up in complex card counting, betting, and strategy systems — just stick to the basic rules of how to play.

3. <u>Cheat Card:</u> For each game, print out a cheat card that shows the basic playing strategy and keep it as a reference guide when you forget.

5 Movies to Watch Before Your Trip:

1. *Swingers:* Learn from Mikey's mistake: Don't go in too hard only to blow your bankroll in a few minutes. Don't let this film give you the misguided belief that you stand half a chance with a Vegas cocktail waitress, because you don't. Stick with the out-of-town honeys and you'll be money.

2. *Casino:* Although it's a bit of a downer, this is pretty much the only way you'll get to see the mob-run Vegas. But it gives you an idea of what things were like in "the good old

days," when you could become the victim of a random act of violence for shooting glances at the wrong guy's doll.

3. *Bugsy:* Looking for a Vegas history lesson? Well, this Barry Levinson flick will have you covered. You'll get to see how a mobster with a dream set everything in motion.

4. *Ocean's Eleven:* Whether you choose the Rat Pack version or the slick remake, they'll get you pumped to bring down the house.

5. *Caddyshack:* When they decide to bet on their golf game …OK, this one's not even remotely tied to Vegas, but it's one of our all-time faves and you should watch it whenever you have the chance.

5 Movies Not to Watch before Your Trip

1. *The Cooler:* Don't depress yourself with demoralizing view of downtown Vegas. This version of Vegas won't get you pumped up.

2. *Leaving Las Vegas:* A man goes to Vegas to drink himself to death. Enough said.

3. *Honeymoon in Vegas:* A romantic comedy about a couple that goes to Vegas to get married. You are going to Vegas to party with the guys, not to dress up like Elvis and propose to your woman.

4. *Ocean's Twelve:* It looks like a Vegas movie sequel, but the whole thing takes place in Europe.

5. *Caddyshack II:* Again, not a Vegas movie. While the original is an all American classic, the Jackie Mason development of a putt-putt course is a downer. Skip.

5 Songs to Bring on Your Trip:

1. <u>Elvis Presley's "Viva Las Vegas"</u>: No one captures the energy of Las Vegas quite like The King.

2. <u>Frank Sinatra's "Luck Be a Lady Tonight"</u>: Maybe Old Blue Eyes' luck will rub off on you; stranger things have happened.

3. <u>Mötley Crüe's "Girls, Girls, Girls"</u>: This strip club staple will get you ready to hit the town.

4. <u>Motorhead's "Ace of Spades"</u>: Listen to this one at eleven.

5. <u>Kenny Rogers's "The Gambler"</u>: No justification needed.

5 Books to Bring on Your Trip:

1. There's really only one you need, and you're reading it.

2. However, if you must, try Ben Mezrich's *Bringing Down the House*, the story of a bunch of MIT geeks who developed a byzantine card counting system and scored some serious money playing blackjack.

3. *Positively Fifth Street* is James McManus's account of betting his book advance to win a spot at the World Series of Poker at Binion's. No-limit Texas hold 'em action.

4. *Super Casino.* Pete Early will show you how Las Vegas was transformed from a dingy desert town to the world's playground.

5. *Fear and Loathing in Las Vegas.* "We were somewhere around Barstow on the edge of the desert when the drugs began to take hold." Hunter S. Thompson's original Gonzo valentine to Vegas madness.

From Takeoff to Landing

When you get to the airport you'll notice the departure gate for Las Vegas is unlike that for any other destination. Just the fact that they're going to Vegas makes people much friendlier than they are at, say, the Tulsa gate. Everyone is heading out to the desert with a dream of easy riches, easy women, late nights and lots of alcohol. Like being in a small town in Europe and running into a fellow American, there's an immediate sense of camaraderie.

Hit the Bar

Check out the airport bar closest to your gate: Perhaps there's a group of gals headed out for a bachelorette party. Strike up a little conversation by asking where they're staying. Drop a few pearls of wisdom from the *Little Black Book* so that they think you're a real insider. Make plans to meet up later that night. When the girls see you later, they will feel comforted that they know someone in Vegas.

Hook a Brother Up

Chances are you and your friends will be scattered throughout the cabin on your flight out. Once the beverage cart rolls your way, buy beers for all of your buddies to get everyone into the party spirit. You only live once. It's a class move, and we're sure they'll get you back later in your trip.

Roll In to Town in Style

Here's how to really get your trip kicked off right. Once your plane touches down, walk by the baggage claim (you don't have anything to pick up, because you only packed a carry-on); you'll see lots of hotel limo drivers standing around with placards for guests they're picking up. This sight usually brings everyone down a bit, because they know they're not high rollers and no one is there to greet them except a massive cab line.

Here's where you hook your friends up. Call ahead and ask a

local limo service for an airport pickup. You'll have a driver waiting to whisk you and the boys off to your hotel in style. The benefits of this one are pretty simple. It'll cost you about $45 for the limo. Compare that to having to get multiple cabs (the most you can fit into one cab is four) and waiting in a really long line.

The key to making this a real event is to not give any of your buddies the heads-up. Trust us, if you call ahead and get everything set up without telling them, they'll be knocked out when they see there's a limo waiting for them. You'll be at your hotel sipping your first drink while all the tourists slug it out in the unending cab line.

$$$ IF MONEY IS NO OBJECT

Private Jet: If you really want to roll into town in style, you gotta go with a Gulfstream. Sure, it'll set you back about $5K an hour for flight time, but man is it worth it. You and the boys kicking back watching some DVDs as you're escorted in complete luxury. It's big bucks, but the Gulfstream is our culture's way of saying, "car and mortgage payments are for suckers — you need to live it up."

Airport Hotel Check-In

Several of the Strip properties have check-in desks at the airport. Be sure to call ahead to see if your hotel offers airport check-in, if it does, use it. Even if there's a line, you'll be saving yourself from a much larger line at your hotel. You can get your keys and head off to the casino straight from the airport, and they'll bring your bags to your room for you.

On Your Marks, Get Set, and Go.

You are finally in Vegas at the beginning of a grand adventure. If this is your first time, it will be overwhelming to you. If it's not your first time, there is always something new. Remember, the *Little Black Book* is your guide — keep it by your side and it won't let you down. If you do wind up blowing some money on something stupid, don't be embarrassed. We've all been there before, we didn't get all of our advice for free, and more than a few things were learned the hard way.

If you plan ahead whenever possible, the next few days will certainly be good ones — even great ones. Keep an eye on your troops, stick with the plan and the good times will follow. There's plenty of fun awaiting you, and you owe it to yourself to soak up everything you can.

Viva Las Vegas

✴ Chapter 4 ✴

Accommodations: Why Where You Stay Is More Important Than You Think

✴ ....

Here's the start to a really, really bad trip to Vegas. You and your friends grab your luggage, hop in a cab, and head to your hotel. In your research you've asked around and been told, "as long as you stay near the Strip, you're fine — it doesn't really matter what hotel you pick." So you booked a hotel at a cheap rate just four blocks off of the Strip. After all, what you guys really need is just someplace to store your luggage and to shower in the mornings; the rest of the time it'll be "party, party, party!" You'll hardly be in your hotel room at all. As your cab cruises toward your hotel, you see it: the Las Vegas Strip. Isn't it beautiful? You get a quick glimpse of your playground as the cab catches the light and zooms across the Strip toward your hotel that's "conveniently located just blocks from the Strip."

It's at this moment that you realize a block in Las Vegas is about the size of five blocks in New York City. Your four-block stumble to the Strip in the desert sun isn't looking like such a quick jaunt anymore. Then, as the cab approaches your hotel, reality sets in even harder. From the outside your hotel looks like a downgraded Motel 6. Inside is even worse, with a three-table casino and a piss-smelling puddle of a pool, and it's starting to look like your smart bargain wasn't such a good choice. You're getting what you paid for.

You chose to save a buck on your hotel 'cause you figured it wouldn't matter, and now it's going to haunt you. You've blown the single biggest decision of your whole trip. Your only option now is to just live with it.

Doing it Right: Which One of You's a Tough Guy?

Most guys think that they're only getting a hotel room out of sheer necessity. Each of them secretly thinks that if it were up to him, he wouldn't get a hotel room at all. They're real men, players. Vegas is a 24 hour town, sleep is for suckers, and they plan to be awake every minute they're in Sin City.

Although we applaud your bravado, we think it's idiotic. At some point, no matter how hard you try, you're going to need to get a good night's sleep. You may think that all you need is a reasonably clean bed to crash on, but you need a lot more than that out of your hotel.

If you don't pick the right place to stay, you'll spend your trip waiting in cab lines, schlepping from property to property looking for something to eat, sitting around a glorified kiddie pool, feeling like a loser, and kicking yourself for going cheap.

Your Hotel: The Center Ring of Your Three-Ring Circus

You need a center of operations for your invasion on Sin City. Your base camp needs to be in the right place to allow your crew to successfully soak every ounce of fun out of this town that your time and money will afford. The hotel is where you'll begin and end each day. It's where you'll meet up for meals and outings — it's not just a crash pad at the end of the day. Where you stay is the center of your Vegas universe.

What to Look For:
House Rules: The 8 Key Considerations

Groups of guys have different needs from everyone else. Is it a couples' hotel, a romantic getaway? Forget it. It doesn't matter how expensive the lobby art exhibit is, it'll do nothing for you. Why do you care if a property ranks four diamonds if there's no place to have some fun? When it comes to choosing a hotel, guys only need to consider these eight things.

1. Location, Location, Location

 Desert Mirage | Nothing in Las Vegas is more deceiving than the distance from one property to the next. "Right next door" can mean a half-mile walk door-to-door. While a half mile seems like no big deal, remember during most months of the year the sun beats down on you like an 800-pound gorilla with a hammer and a bad attitude. So, if the hotel you've chosen says "just three blocks away from the Strip," assume that you're going to have to do a lot of walking. Instead, choose a hotel that's in the heart of the action. Nothing sobers you up quite like a two-mile walk back to your room at the end of a long night.

❖ You Can't Get There from Here | One argument for not paying to stay in the center of the action is that you can always take a cab. That's true, if you can find one. Although every hotel has a taxi stand, during a busy weekend night the lines are long. And, if you're lucky enough to actually snag a cab, expect to be sitting comfortably in the backseat for some time, as traffic can be brutal, especially on the Strip; especially when you're in a hurry to get to where the women are. More often than not the money you'll have to spend on taxis to and from your hotel would have paid for a room at a more convenient, upgraded casino.

❖ I Can't Find My Way Out! | Hotels with easy entrances and exits are important. It's no good if your hotel is in the epicenter of Vegas if it takes you twenty minutes to negotiate your way out to the Strip. Some places are downright cavernous, making you want to head straight for the bar when you can't find the door (not a bad idea). Just for fun, try walking through Excalibur without getting lost. It's impossible.

2. Image: You Are Where You Stay

Because every hotel generally attracts a different type of guest, you should choose a place that's full of *your* type of people. You're probably going to spend more time at your hotel than you'd like to admit; that said, make sure you're staying and playing with a crowd that will add fuel to your adventure, not remind you of everything you left at home. The Bellagio crowd is well-heeled and reserved. The Westward Ho crowd is rowdy, raunchy and recently paroled. You can pick one of these, or find a place that lies somewhere in between.

Remember, you *are* where you stay. The first question that you will be asked when talking to other people in town is "Where are you staying?" If you mention a lame hotel, the ladies will think you're a loser. (Note: If you do get stuck at a

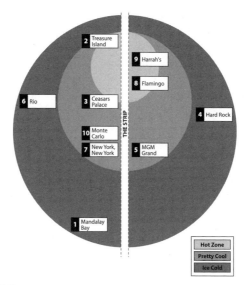

The Hot Zone

This map will help show you the Hot Zone of the Strip.

☘ Hot Zone:

The Hot Zone is the center of the action. Within it are a lot of options, allowing you gambling, dining, and partying at a variety of locations that are only a short walk.

☘ Pretty Cool:

The Pretty Cool Zone provides access to a large variety of options, but requires more effort and resourcefulness on your part. Put your walking shoes on.

☘ Ice Cold:

Get a car, because walking isn't much of an option. This is no indictment of the properties within the Ice Cold Zone because some of them are very good. Unfortunately, their location will really require you to rent your own car, cab it, or get a limo if you want to leave the property (which you will need to do at some point).

less than desirable hotel, be sure to lie when you answer this question). When you head home and tell people about your trip they'll ask where you stayed. Few great stories begin with the line "We stayed at The Riviera . . ."

3. 24-Hour Food: Good, Available Options are a Must

There are tons of places to eat in Las Vegas, but when you're really hungry there had better be a few right in front of you. Wherever you choose to stay has to have a few decent places to grab a quick bite.

The casino's coffee shop will be the center of your food universe. It's the place where you will start when you wake up, and the place you will end up drunk at five in the morning. A bad coffee shop will quickly bring you down, so a 24-hour dining establishment with good food and good service is a must. Casinos are required by law to serve food round the clock, but some choose to grossly understaff the late night to early morning shifts. This means at some casinos it could take you forever to get your food, when all you really want is something to eat before you pass out.

A Good Coffee Shop Must-Have

- ❀ A clean and pleasant atmosphere. A place where you will enjoy spending a hour whether you are in a party mood or hung over.

- ❀ Timely service. You will get real hungry in Vegas (we don't know why this is so; maybe the desert air, late nights, constant action, whatever), so you want to have a place where you can chow down quickly. Coffee shops aren't exactly an epicurean experience. They exist to fill your stomach quickly.

- ❀ Good, tasty food in reasonable portion.

4. The Center Bar: Putting You in the Middle of the Action

Every good hotel needs a good bar that serves as your base camp of hotel operations. You will use the center bar more than you think. It's the place you tell people to meet up with you, it's a meeting place when you are going out as a group, it's a place to grab a quick cocktail after check-in, and it's a place you can go to step away from the casino action and breathe. It's also a place where the non-gamblers can have a good time while their friends are still working the tables. And, most importantly, it is a place where women tend to end up when they can't find any other viable options. It is easier to meet a girl at a bar than walking around the casino floor.

A Good Center Bar Must-Have

- ❧ It must be an accessible and convenient area with a good vantage point for the entire casino. This is the base camp, you should not struggle to get there.

- ❧ It must have large tables where a group can sit. You will need to sit and talk while waiting for your friends. You can't talk to a group when you're sitting at a bar, so comfortable table seating is key.

- ❧ It needs to be accessible, yet removed. You don't want to be part of the casino, but slightly removed from the action. Just enough that you can always step in and out of the chaos going on around you.

- ❧ It must have a view of people passing by. An elevated center bar with a sight line of people coming toward and away from you is ideal. Then you can look at passersby without staring them down. Plus, the sooner you can see them, the more time you have to come up with a way to meet them. Don't keep your back to the action — angle so you have a view.

♣ It must have cocktail servers, the hotter and friendlier the better. The key is to get these girls on your side. They have more power than you think to slip you a couple of drinks, on the side, free of charge. Also, they can help you meet women. So be nice and generous to your cocktail server.

♣ It mustn't get too crowded. A good center bar allows you to carry on a conversation in a happening environment. If people are bumping against you and the music is blaring, you might as well be in a night club. A good center bar is one that's popular, but not too popular.

5. Nightlife: A Place for the Masses

A good hotel needs nightlife that appeals to the average Joe. It has to be easy to get into, and be a place where people are having fun, Vegas style, which usually means a cheesy bar with a Vegas lounge band. Cheesy bars are populated with groups of girls that aren't your typical nightclub types. These gals are not about attitude. They are in the mood to party with you. Without a place like this in your hotel, you don't stand much of a chance with the ladies. "Let's head up to our suite" is a much easier sell than "lets go stand in this cab line, we'll have you back to our hotel in less than two hours!"

Essential Features of a Good Nightclub:

♣Easy access for a group of guys to get into. Tired of waiting in a line for a nightclub where they only let in women and the guys who tip them $100? Then don't. Your time is precious, so don't wait around in a line.

♣A cover charge that is not too hefty. Expect some sort of cover charge, but nothing too pricey. Anywhere from $5 to $10 is OK, but once you go over $20, forget it.

♣Relaxed dress code. You are looking for a place that attracts people out for a good time, not a stuffy club where people are looking to see a celebrity. Look for nightspots where people are wearing relaxed clothes. Chances are the woman there are a lot easier to meet than elsewhere.

♣Entertainment that gets the crowd going.

♣Some type of common area where you can hang out, talk, and meet women.

♣Loud, but not too loud. The music must be low enough that you can carry on a conversation but loud enough to create energy.

♣A dance floor where people don't care what they are doing. There's nothing worse than being on a dance floor filled with people who actually know how to dance. You need to feel free to do the Cabbage Patch and not look like an idiot (well, perhaps that's pushing it).

6. The Pool: Fun in the Sun

One of the best reasons to buck up for a decent hotel is to have access to its pool. Most guys make a huge mistake when they plan their trip by not even considering what they're going to do during the daylight hours. The pool is the daytime nerve center of your hotel. It is where groups of girls hang around in varying states of undress, sipping umbrella drinks, and just waiting to meet guys. The pool is reserved for hotel guests only. If you aren't staying at the hotel, they're happy to take your money in the casino, but they'll be damned if they're going to let you use their pool. If you choose the right place to stay, you can rent a cabana, play blackjack poolside, check out some serious female talent, or relax in a wave pool or tube down a lazy river. If you go cheap, you can forget all of this.

Note Vegas pools are closed from November to March, so don't worry about this one during the winter time.

7. Sportsbook: Think of It as a Pool for the Winter Time

For those of you who don't know Vegas, a sportsbook is the place to make bets and watch sports. You can place legal wagers on pretty much any sporting event around the country here. When it's cold outside you'll probably have a lot of time on your hands during the day. Easy access to a good sportsbook can chase those hangover blues away. Comfy chairs, good food, and lots of TV sets are exactly what you need on game day. Few things top spending the afternoon kicking back the Heinekens while watching football games in an exciting environment.

8. Facility: Cleanliness Counts

You want to stay at a hotel that's clean and well-maintained. No one wants to stay at a place that looks like it belongs in dingy old Atlantic City. This is Vegas: your hotel should be in good shape. Places can look old really fast here; they'll blow them up before they will remodel them. If the hotel facilities aren't well maintained you'll feel like you're getting ripped off, and if you wanted to feel like that you'd just spring for a bottle at an ultra lounge.

🍸 Classic Vegas Mistake

Not so Hot Tubbin': Having a Jacuzzi tub in the middle of your suite sounds pretty sweet. Well, it's not. Although it's a nice option for a romantic weekend, it's no fun to see one of your friends lying naked in boiling water at five a.m. We know what you're thinking: "If we get the Jacuzzi, we'll be able to get some girls to head up to the room with us." Trust us, any girl who's willing to go up to your room with you is willing to go up to your room with you — the Jacuzzi will not be the determining factor. Lots of guys go this route and spend half their trip trying to convince women to head up to their room for some hot tubbing. Plus, a Jacuzzi takes up a lot of space that you'll probably need based on the number of people you'll have staying in the room, not to mention it's loud as hell and takes forever to fill up.

Choose Wisely

Rank the eight criteria based on importance to your group. If it is wintertime, the pool is a non-factor. Below are the *Little Black Book*'s Top 10 hotels for groups of guys. Use the following chart to determine which one is right for you.

May–October	Location	Image	Eating	Center Bar	Nightlife	Pool	Sportsbook	Facility	TOTALS
Mandalay Bay	3	10	7	7	6	10	9	10	62
Treasure Island	8	8	7	10	9	6	4	9	61
Caesars	9	7	8	9	6	7	7	7	60
Hard Rock	1	10	10	6	4	8	10	10	59
MGM Grand	5	7	8	9	5	9	8	7	58
Rio	5	7	8	5	10	8	5	7	55
NY–NY	5	7	7	6	10	1	10	8	54
Flamingo	10	4	4	3	7	9	3	4	44
Harrah's	10	5	4	4	10	2	4	5	44
Monte Carlo	5	6	7	2	7	5	3	6	41

November–April (pool is not a factor)	Location	Image	Eating	Center Bar	Nightlife	Sportsbook	Facility	TOTALS
Treasure Island	8	8	7	10	9	4	9	55
NY–NY	5	7	7	6	10	10	8	53
Caesars	9	7	8	9	6	7	7	53
Mandalay Bay	3	10	7	7	6	9	10	52
Hard Rock	1	10	10	6	4	10	10	51
MGM Grand	5	7	8	9	5	8	7	49
Rio	5	7	8	5	10	5	7	47
Harrah's	10	5	4	4	10	4	5	42
Monte Carlo	5	6	7	2	7	3	6	36
Flamingo	10	4	4	3	7	3	4	35

1. Mandalay Bay: A Class Act

The theme at Mandalay Bay is kind of hard to pin down. It claims to be a forbidden city in an exotic jungle island centered around a lagoon. Whatever that means. Mandalay's events center has brought a lot of convention business to the south end of The Strip. Mandalay has a lot to offer, but it's not cheap, and it's location makes getting anywhere difficult.

Location

Terrible. Taxis are a must. The only route by foot is through Luxor and Excalibur. Mandalay does not have an exit onto the Strip. If you have a rental, use the valet inside the back parking garage. Location is the only real drawback to what's an otherwise amazing property.

Image

You've got money and aren't afraid to spend it.

24-Hour Food

The food quality, décor, and service are excellent at Raffles. The tables are not on top of one another, so there will be room to talk. Ask for a table in the back; tables at the entrance have traffic passing by right next to them. Great menu items are the omelets, the chicken Caesar, and barbecue chicken. You will enjoy your meal.

Center Bar

The Island Lounge in the middle of the casino. It is a nice squared-shaped bar with a jazz band. The bar is cut off from the casino a little too much, so you can't really people watch. There are tables and cocktail service, but you won't find many unescorted women hanging out here.

Nightlife

The Coral Lounge gets going after 10 p.m. It is an easy place to dance with girls but a tough place to socialize at the tables because of its awkward layout. So hit the dance floor hard — you will always find a group of girls dancing together. House of Blues is another option. Cheesy 70s and 80s tribute bands play there every weekend. The Coral Lounge and House of Blues are the only places you have a chance of scoring in Mandalay. The other nightlife options of Rumjungle, Mix, and Foundation Room are the types of upscale nightclubs that have no interest in letting in a group of guys. They want to maintain a high girl-to-guy ratio, so don't bother unless you have some girls with you already.

Pool

A massive tourist pool, the likes of which you would find at a family resort. It is always packed. Hang out at the pool bar and grab a seat under an umbrella. At the far end of the pool area is the exclusive topless pool Moorea Beach. Expect to pony up to enter this pool. Do not venture there with a group of more than two guys unless you want the women to catch a glimpse of you, think they're being invaded by Huns, and quickly put their tops back on.

Sportsbook

Massive, but can quickly get overcrowded. Cocktail service is excellent on lighter sports days. During the play-offs, avoid it like the plague, it's just too crowded.

Facility

Perfect. Mandalay is a hip, upscale setting with no real drawbacks. Room quality is superb, especially in the new tower called THEhotel.

2. TI, (The Hotel Formerly Known as Treasure Island): A Sure Thing

Treasure Island junked its pirate theme for something completely different: a female pirate theme. The focus is no longer on swashbucklers. Now it's on swashbucklers in leather bustiers. Gone is the establishment's family focus, to be replaced with a distinctly adult vibe. There is a lot to like about this place, no matter what they're calling it.

Location

It's in the Hot Zone, with easy access to other properties, such as the Venetian, Wynn, and the funky fun of the New Frontier and Casino Royale. TI is not that big, so it's easy to negotiate your way through the casino.

Image

Cool, young, hip, and laid back.

24-Hour Food

The Terrace Café. Good, clean, but somewhat crowded. It has the standard coffee shop menu. For breakfast, be sure to order the B.B.C. omelet: It's apple-smoked bacon, broccoli, and cheddar cheese — a modern classic. During the day the Mexican restaurant Isla and Canter's Delicatessen are good food alternatives.

Center Bar

The Breeze Bar. Grab a seat around the perimeter of the bar; the best spot is the corner by the Terrace Café. You want to be able to see people walking by, maybe make some eye contact. The bar's got TVs with sports, so there is always something to distract you if your friend starts in on one of his famous drunken rants.

Nightlife

The Kaunaville bar is about as cheesy a Vegas experience as

you can get. This is a great place to hang out between 9 p.m. and midnight, Wednesday to Saturday, when Cirque du Soleil's *Mystère* lets out. The *Mystère* crowd is usually pretty tired, and they need to have their batteries recharged. So make your move quick with the girls and bring a lot of energy. Sit at the front left side of the bar, the section that faces the door. The bartenders here will help you out: They want to get the crowd pumped up before it decides it's pooped out. The best play is to send a group of girls a round of shots (try the Purple Hooters). The bartender will set up a display of shots and employ some slick moves out of the movie **Cocktail** to wow the girls. Then, you can swoop right in and start talking. Kaunaville also features that fun, cheesy Vegas staple: dueling pianos every night at 10 p.m.

Pool
Solid pool. Although there are better pools out there, this one should provide you with a good time. It has a huge, fifty-person Jacuzzi that serves as the socialization center. Grab a seat away from the middle and make rounds to the Jacuzzi anytime you see some girls there.

Sportsbook
Six faded large screens and four normal TVs. Thirty-six total seats. Dead atmosphere tucked away in the corner of the casino by Tangerine. No cocktail service in sight. If you want to watch sports, go to the bar at Isla, the Mexican restaurant.

Facility
Newly remodeled in 2004, TI is a clean, well-lit property with high quality décor. The rooms are average in size and have quality, traditional furnishings. The best rooms face the Strip and have a spectacular view of the nightly pirate show.

3. Caesars Palace: The Romans Have the Basics Covered

Caesars is legendary, which until recently meant old. In the last few years, however, Caesars has undergone a series of expansions and upgrades. This once-faded beauty has added some nightlife that has attracted a younger crowd to what used to be a Grecian Formula establishment.

Location

Right in the middle of the Hot Zone, with easy access by foot and taxi to many different venues. On the downside, it's big and the layout is confusing, so give yourself some time to learn your way around or expect to be walking in circles.

Image

Classy, but be prepared for a few "Are you going to Celine Dion?" jokes at your expense.

24-Hour Food

Café Lago. This nice coffee shop is newly remodeled. It's located in the back part of the casino by the pool. It's bright, though — so bright that your buzz turns into a migraine faster than you can say "Hail Caesar!" But it is spacious and offers a sense of privacy, so your drunk-ass friend can talk about the stripper he swears is in love with him without everyone overhearing. The food quality is solid, but avoid the traditional breakfast hours, as the line becomes swollen with all the soon-to-be blue-hairs who line up for eggs over easy and Cream of Wheat.

Center Bar

The Seahorse Lounge is one of the best center bars around. If you walk through the main entrance, it is on your right, on the way to the sportsbook. This is one of the only center bars that doesn't have video poker, a big plus when trying to talk to girls. It is clean, it always has cocktail service, plenty of places to sit, and it has house music pumped in to create a little atmosphere. Their drink menu is great here because they serve pitchers of mixed drinks. When you order a girl a drink, order one of these to share. It also has an appetizer menu with sushi and chocolate fondue, so you can go really *Swingers* cheesy if you want to. Also, it has a $23 bottle of champagne that you can send to a group of ladies without breaking the bank. Do it up and use this place as command central.

Nightlife
Cleopatra's Barge. We love it! This dance floor barge gets happening around 10 p.m. This is real Las Vegas cheese: DJ music and a dance floor that moves and billows with theatrical smoke. The party crowd at Cleopatra's is a little older than some of the other hot spots, so don't expect to find any 21 year-olds here.

Pool
A decent pool with a couple of different levels. It's a great place to hang out and people-watch, so bring your sunglasses. Order the huge glass half-yard daiquiris (they come complete with a neck strap so you won't drop it). The half-yard will keep your refill runs to a minimum. Plus, because of their size, the half-yards make excellent props to talk to girls; they make you out to be a fun, friendly, and non-intimidating guy.

Sportsbook
A pretty good sportsbook, though unfortunately it's a bit too big for its own good. There are two huge screens dedicated to sports, but they would look better if the lights were dimmed a bit more. Avoid the large screens and set up at one of the cocktail tables that has a TV on it. This is one of the few sportsbooks where they have sound going, so if you are able to score one of the cocktail tables, you'll be all set. Cocktail service is good, the service prompt. Be sure to ask for drink vouchers when you make a bet.

Facility

A mixed bag: some good, some bad. Although there are some great parts of Caesars, the old Centurion Tower is old — really old. The rooms in this tower are about the size of a bathroom and offer only a view of the towers that you should have requested a room in.

4. Hard Rock: Sometimes Size Doesn't Matter

Hard Rock is a boutique hotel. What does that mean to you? It means it's small and you probably can't afford it. Seriously, this nicely appointed, rock-and-roll-themed establishment is loud and cool. It's a great little hotel that has a lot of things going for it. Unfortunately, location isn't one of them.

Location

Way out there. Getting anywhere is a pain in the neck. A rental car is key if you choose to stay here. Unlike other hotels, Hard Rock is small and compact, so it's easy to get from your room to the casino.

Image

Staying here says you're a player.

24-Hour Food

Mr. Lucky's is the best coffee shop in town. You'll get great food, impeccable service and fun atmosphere 24 hours a day. It's the only coffee shop social enough that you might even be able to strike up a conversation with some women. Try the Secret Special: $7.77 steak-and -shrimp combo, it's a New York Strip Steak, three jumbo garlic sautéed shrimp, mashed potatoes, and a salad. This off-the-menu special is a sure thing.

Center Bar

Although most people think the Hard Rock center bar is the best in town, we think it leaves a lot to be desired. First, there are no tables to sit at. If you want to sit, you have to sit at the bar, facing inward, leaving you with no opportunity to watch the ladies. Second, there are no cocktail servers. You have to fight your way up to the bar to get a drink. Third, it gets way too crowded. On a Friday or Saturday night, it's overwhelming.

Nightlife

There is no nightlife for a group of guys. You'll end up walking around in circles, not really knowing where to go, or fighting for a drink at the center bar. Your best bet is to hang out at the bar in the Pink Taco.

Pool

It is a grand pool, but you'd better look good. The girls are hot, and the guys are buff musclemen. Your best bet is to grab a seat at the bar in the middle. It's in the shade, so you won't be embarrassed to keep your shirt on. Here, you can grab some drinks, some good food, and you can get an eyeful of the hot cocktail servers who work here. You don't want to hang out with a large group of guys because it will be difficult to mingle. Three is perfect. Bring a paper, so you can talk sports with your buddies and not get caught up just staring at the beautiful talent. Even better, bring your copy of the *Little Black Book* and look like the player you are.

Sportsbook

A small, intimate, sportsbook. No line for wagering, great cocktail service, and never too crowded.

Facility

Although it could stand to be freshened up, the facilities are overall pretty nice. The room décor, bed, and furniture make you feel like you are staying in a hip, plush L.A. hotel. Having a room here means you will enjoy your stay and feel like a player.

5. MGM Grand: Grand Yes, But Give Me Some Nightlife

The MGM Grand is an enormous property that boasts over 5,000 rooms. This Hollywood-themed establishment pays homage to its company's proud cinema heritage, complete with a yellow brick road and a habitat for the MGM lions. The "City of Entertainment," which really is as big as your average small city, has a wide variety of accommodation options at several price points. From standard rooms to Skylofts, their exclusive hotel within the hotel, there is a room for everyone. Make sure you request the Grand Tower, which is home to the larger, newer rooms. One thing working against the MGM Grand is its size. It just seems to go on forever. Although you may get lost, it will meet your needs.

Location

Pretty cool. It's difficult to exit to the Strip, and once you do make it outside, the only two casinos close to you are Tropicana and New York-New York. You have a ways to walk to get anywhere else. Expect to cab it a lot.

Image

Not so great, but it will do. Everyone is clean-cut and conservative, so it's not really a party crowd. It gets crowded at night, so your group should be prepared to walk in a single file line through the throng. The floor plan is not as confusing as some other casinos', so at least you won't lose your group if you turn your head.

24-Hour Food

The Studio Café. You do not want to find yourself here during the late night. Bright lights, slow service, and — to add insult to injury — usually a wait to get in. With over 5,000 rooms and only one 24-hour restaurant, there is often a substantial line. Do yourself a favor: Go to your room and order room service.

Center Bar

The MGM is so grand that it has two center bars. The Kuri bar is located near the lobby of the casino, and the Centrifuge bar is located in the rotunda at the entrance to the Strip. The only drawbacks are that they both get pretty crowded, making it difficult to get a seat or a drink at times. Both are elevated, giving you a good vantage point, and there's just enough separation between you and the casino floor so that people don't think you're staring at them. Drink prices are a little high, but if you get a good seat, it's worth it.

Nightlife

Not really anything here for the average guy. This place is filled with high-end bottle service places like Tabu and Teatro. These ultramodern ultra lounges only want the type of guys who bring women with them and are going to buy expensive bottles. Studio 54, a huge, loud dance club, is also tough for a group of guys to get into. If you do get in, you will find yourself fighting to get a drink and separated from your buddies. Your best bet is to hang out at the bar inside Wolfgang Puck's, which is the restaurant of choice for ladies. Wait until they are finishing their food, and walk on over. Most of the time these girls are looking for something to do for the night. The only other options are the center bars or the Television City Bar, which is the daiquiri bar on the exit ramp to New York–New York. The line for Studio 54 goes right next to this bar, so you may be able to convince some girls to join you at your table instead of waiting in line.

Pool

Huge, very nice pool. There are several different sections, so you can always switch it up if the section you are in gets lame. The best place to meet women is the lazy river. It moves just slow enough for you to talk and walk around the pool.

Sportsbook

Newly built, the sportsbook is top of the line. The book has a huge wall of plasma TVs, many chairs and booths, cocktail service, and plenty of betting windows. It is also very close to the Centrifuge center bar, making it a great place to watch a game while keeping close to the social action.

Facility

The place smells like carpet freshener, the one you used in your college dorm room just before your parents came for a visit. It's like they put it on the floor and forgot to vacuum it up. This place is big, really big. If you get a room at the end of the long tower, be sure to have your walking shoes on. Be kind to yourself and be sure to ask for a room close to the elevator.

$$$IF MONEY IS NO OBJECT

The Mansion at MGM: Looking for a place to stay and got 5K? Then look no further. That's right, for a mere $5,000 a night you can get yourself a two-bedroom villa at this very exclusive, very private lodging. The prices go up from there (north of $17,000 for the biggest suite on a holiday weekend), but you get a lot for your money (sort of) including your own butler and antique-furnished rooms. Besides, you get access to a private pool so you don't have to worry about getting up early to get a good lounge chair. No need to wait in the cab line — a Rolls-Royce will be waiting to pick you up at the airport. Don't make the mistake of getting a little out of control; that painting you accidentally knocked off the wall just might be a Picasso.

---

6. Rio: Proof That There's Life off the Strip

It's Carnivale every day at Rio. Okay maybe not exactly Carnivale, but there are beads being tossed around, and the atmosphere is decidedly loose and jazzed. Located off the

Strip, Rio is an "all suites" hotel with a Carnivale theme. Masquerade Village, their shopping plaza, hosts a sky carnival several times a day: That's right, giant parade floats move along a track high above your head. With good rooms, a good pool, and a great nightlife you'll just wish it were on the Strip.

Location

While most think the Rio is too far away from the Strip, it is a much better location than hotels like Mandalay Bay and Luxor and is closer than the other off-Strip hotels like the Hard Rock. It's just a short cab ride away from the Hot Zone. Don't take the shuttle or attempt to walk from here. The shuttle takes forever, and you will be on a packed bus with a bunch of seniors. If you walk, you have to cross over an interstate. If you drive here, be sure to park in the surface lot near Bikini's Nightclub or you will end up dragging bags through the casino. It takes a little while to get your bearings in this casino; there are not a lot of points of reference, and your sight lines are short. It is also one of the few casinos that is within walking distance of a strip club. Just down the street on Valley View is Striptease. If you don't take a cab, you will probably be able to talk your way in through the door for free. Cabbies will offer you a free ride there, but if you take it, then there is no way to get in for free. The clubs kickback the cabbies $20 for dropping someone off, then pass the cost on to you at the door.

Image

You like to party, but don't have a ton of cash. The place breeds an all around good time. People are in good moods here, and you won't find the lowlife element that occupies some parts of the Strip.

24-Hour Food

Sao Paulo is good, but it's a little bit off the beaten path. You can find it by heading toward the Penn & Teller Theater. Your best bet is to stick with the Asian menu; the omelets and other dishes are a little too pricey.

Center Bar
The true center bar is Ibar. It has good points and bad points. First, it has places to sit and people-watch. There are plasma TVs around the bar, so you won't get too bored. The bad part is that it's usually empty — I mean really empty. I once sat in here for an hour before another person walked in. The drink prices make you feel like you are in New York City: $15 for a martini. Ouch! Another choice for a center bar is the Masquerade Bar, but it's only open at night. Nestled between the casino and the Masquerade Village, Masquerade has an elevated vantage point with long sight lines to check out the hotties as they approach.

Nightlife
Voodoo Lounge is a perfect place for a group of guys. Hang out outside, drink to excess, and dance drunk with the girls. They have a lounge band inside and a DJ on the outdoor patio. The best time to get there is right before the Chippendales show lets out, since most of the women are all wound up and heading up to Voodoo. To help out on the price of admission, plus get a show, look around for showgirls handing out two-for-one flyers to the show Erotica. The show costs $34.95 — $17.50 each with your flyer. Your ticket stub then gets you free admission to Voodoo and Club Rio, which usually cost $20 at the door. So just by buying the tickets, you save over $5 on two admissions to Voodoo, and you can watch Erotica if you like. It's a mix between hard rock music and an adult review. Put your savings to good use at the bar.

Pool
A good party pool, but not the most immaculate by far. Hang out at the Coco Cabana Bar on the left-hand side if you want to meet some girls. If you are going by the pool for sun, be

sure to get out there early. The hotel tower cuts off the sunlight in the afternoon. Plan on moving around a couple times to stay in the rays.

Sportsbook
One of the smallest sportsbooks possible, thanks to the poker room they made out of the right-hand side of the race and sports. It is smoke-filled, with one hundred chairs that look like they belong in a junior high auditorium (complete with the little attached writing desks). You don't want to hang here and watch a game. There are six rinky-dink TVs dedicated to the sports book, and the rest is for race. It is located next to Toscano's Deli, which is a great place to get a quick bite.

Facility
Pretty good shape. The new tower (the tall one) is nicer in room quality than the old one. Each room is a petite suite with a pullout couch that serves as an extra bed.

7. New York–New York: The Sun Don't Shine in the Big Apple
Once you get past the fact that this NYC-themed property really isn't like New York at all (no one is asking for handouts, and there doesn't seem to be a hot dog stand or a guy selling fake Prada purses in sight), New York–New York is actually pretty cool. With several accommodation options, moderately priced rooms and a decent quotient of good-looking girls, New York–New York has a lot to offer.

Location
Pretty cool — you can walk to Monte Carlo or MGM pretty easily. If you are driving here and need to check in, be sure to park on the third floor of the parking garage on the side facing the Excalibur. There is a bridge that brings you over to the hotel, right near the registration. The other bridge will drop you off in the arcade, which is full of kids and difficult to maneuver through after you've had a few.

Image

A fun, easygoing crowd that's clean-cut but not overly fancy. The people here like to party, they just can't last all night.

24-Hour Food

The coffee shop, America, while open 24 hours, only offers a limited late-night menu during the wee hours that lacks most off the good stuff. The place has super-high ceilings and is dead quiet at night, so you kind of feel like you are eating in a vast warehouse.

Center Bar

New York–New York lacks a center bar, so you'll have to find another place to hang during the day. One of the real problems with New York–New York is that the floor plan has no true center. Although there's no center bar, at night there are a bunch of venues that open up for a good time

Nightlife

There are plenty of options. The Bar at Times Square known as the Piano bar is the best option. When you enter, go to the left and stand — you want to be able to move around as you talk to the girls. If you choose to sit at the right of the entrance you'll get locked in, unable to move. The Big Apple bar gears up after midnight on Friday and Saturday with the cheesiest of DJs from midnight to 6 a.m. The small dance floor gets packed, so jump in. During the day on the top of the escalators leading to MGM Grand there's a daiquiri bar where many girls stop to buy drinks. Hang out here and strike up a conversation on what concoction they are drinking and where they are going next.

Pool

If this place had anything that resembled a pool, it would have more of a top ranking all around. The outdoor action is nothing more than a kiddie pool in the middle of a parking lot. The sun doesn't even hit it because it is wedged in between the hotel tower and the parking garage leaving you with the type of lounging experience you'd expect on a fall day in Manhattan.

Sportsbook
The actual sportbook here is awful, but is located next to the ESPN Zone, which is usually a great place to watch a game.

Facility
Good, but not great. The casino environment is well-maintained and intimate, making this a nice place to gamble or have a drink. On the hotel side, the standard rooms vary in size, so be sure to ask for the largest available.

On the Cusp – Three Runners-Up
These three hotels are worth considering when you can't get into the top seven. Although they shouldn't be considered top-tier choices, each does have its strengths.

8. Flamingo: Great Location But . . .
The Flamingo's location can't be beat. Right in the middle of the action with easy access to the Strip and other casinos in the area. But this place lacks both image and food options. So don't eat, or tell anyone you are staying here. Although, "the house that Bugsy built" has definitely seen better days, the reasonable rates often attract a good amount of younger folk.

Location
Perfect. Right in the middle of the Hot Zone, with easy access to the Strip.

Image
Less than desirable. It's no place to brag about.

24-Hour Food

The Tropical Beach Café. Located down by the pool on the left-hand side. We can't vouch for all of the options; if you eat here, stick with the basics.

Center Bar

No center bar exists; the closest thing is the Garden Bar, which is the sunken bar past the sportsbook on your way to the pool. It does have cocktail servers, but lacks the view and character of a good center bar.

Nightlife

Margaritaville is your option. Stay at the bar until 11 p.m. and then hit the dance floor when they move the dining tables. It gets really crowded and fun here during spring break.

Pool

Huge fun pool, which gets crowded. Get out to the pool early, as after 10 a.m. you'll have trouble finding a lounger.

Sportsbook

Average-size TVs with sixteen chairs. Right behind the chairs are slot machines with the sound turned way up. Not really a great place to watch games. During play-offs and big games they do sometimes convert the tour lobby into a viewing area. It is located at the very end of the restaurant row hallway, but it's still not worth your time. Take advantage of the property's great location and go somewhere else to watch a game.

Facility

Old, real old. The pool grounds are well-maintained, but the rest of the property needs to be freshened up a bit.

9. Harrahs: Cheesy Vegas Nightlife Baby!

Don't confuse Harrah's Mardi Gras theme with Rio's Carnivale theme. Although they are part of the same parent company, there's a big difference between the two. Rio is tropical, Brazilian, exotic. Harrah's is Bourbon Street, New Orleans, dirty. Although Harrah's is not squeaky clean, by any stretch of the imagination, it is fun and affordable.

Location
Almost perfect. Just up the street from Flamingo. Quick access to the Strip but slow access to taxis, because the taxi stand is on the back side.

Image
If you stay here you're saying, "We couldn't find anywhere else to stay."

24-Hour Food
Harrah's has the standard Vegas coffee shop. It will do but it won't blow you away.

Center Bar
No true center bar. During the day, the piano bar is where you should just chill and have some drinks. The piano bar is located near the entrance, so you do get a good view of people walking by, but nobody really stops in the place during the day.

Nightlife
The king of the cheese. You will meet more available drunk girls here than anywhere else. Between the Carnival Court and the Piano bar, it is a haven for the ladies.

Pool
Second-floor Holiday Inn pool with the smell of chlorine. Avoid.

Sportsbook

Weak; it's mostly dedicated to the horseplayers. There is a bar to grab a decent bite and watch games, so if you have to, end up here.

Facility

Weak, but improving. They are always taking steps to develop the facility, but Harrah's, like Flamingo, was built in the old Vegas style before the mega resorts, and there's only so much they can do.

10. Monte Carlo: Save Me with a Brew at the Pub

This casino-themed property doesn't pack everything that the *Black Book* crowd is looking for. There's a reason it's at the bottom of the list. Yes, it's worth staying here, but if you can find a room elsewhere, perhaps you should. The real redeeming factor of this middle-of-the-road establishment is its brewpub.

Location

Pretty cool. It is a decent walk both ways on the Strip to another casino. The road behind Monte Carlo, Frank Sinatra Drive, makes the hotel taxi-friendly to get to other parts of the Strip without actually going onto the Strip.

Image

Bland. This is a nondescript place full of nondescript people.

24-Hour Food

Called the "Café," it offers an adequate selection of food. It's clean, has comfortable furniture, and the food is fair to good enough.

Center Bar

The Houdini Lounge. On the right-hand side to the casino, this bar is the most boring bar we've ever been to. It's smoke-filled, and lacks the qualities of a good center bar.

Nightlife

The Monte Carlo Brew Pub usually has a decent crowd. The beer, food, and the atmosphere here are all pretty good. Don't wait in line for a table, proceed directly to the bar to the left.

Pool

A dinky pool that is one of the only pools in Vegas to be heated, so it does have the advantage of being open year round. No one really uses it during the winter months, but it is always nice to have the option.

Sportsbook

Eight tiny TVs with a couple of chairs. It looks like this place really only cares about the ponies. Head to the Brewpub if you want to watch a game; they put the big games up on a big screen.

Facility

Looks grungy from the outside; the inside is better. Rooms are solid but not over the top. The Hyper Market has the best liquor selection around. Located at the entrance from the Strip beside New York–New York, it's open until midnight and has every liquor, wine, and beer selection you are looking for. Even if you are just walking by the Monte Carlo, it is a good idea to pop in and buy a bottle or a six-pack.

No Place Has It All

One mistake that many Vegas newcomers make is trying to find the one place that has it all. No single property has everything you're looking for in your trip. We have yet to find a Strip hotel casino that leaves you with no reason to go off property. While it's important to take where you stay seriously, know that there is no be-all and end-all. Remember: None of the hotels have strip joints right in them, so you're going to have to leave at least once! This is Vegas — you want to get out and see the sights, but just make sure your lodgings meet your needs.

> **Note: Properties That Didn't Make the Cut**
>
> You've probably noticed that several well-known, very good properties aren't on the Top 10. Places like the Wynn, Bellagio, the Venetian, the Palms, and Paris are great places to stay; however, they are not ideal for groups of guys. If you don't have lots of money, then Bellagio and Wynn aren't for you, and if you're not with your wife, avoid Paris. All of these places come up short on the *Black Book* matrix of guys' criteria. So, while the Lucky 7 list is not definitively the 7 best hotels in Las Vegas, it is absolutely the 7 best hotels for groups of guys.

Venturing Away from the Lucky 7

If you choose to stay at a place that isn't on the Lucky 7, you might regret it. There are lots of other great places to stay in Vegas, but none of them will be a homerun with your group. Remember: If you decide to stay elsewhere, do your homework and use the 8 keys for finding a good hotel as your guidelines. Ignore them at your own peril.

How to Get the Best Room Rates

❧ Start on their Web site. Many hotels will give their best rate on the Web site because it costs them less money to book someone electronically.

❧ Call the central reservation numbers and ask how much for a suite. You stand a fair chance at being upgraded from a regular room to a suite at check-in. However, although it's pricey, if you're not a Vegas regular you might want to book a suite just to be sure.

In Case You're Asking: Why do you stand a good chance at getting a suite upgrade? If you think that casino regulars get their suites comped, you're wrong. Few players merit a suite; many get free rooms, but to get a suite, you have to play some real dollars. The casino hosts get angry if the hotel gives a free room player a suite upgrade, because they want the player to earn the suite. Otherwise, they give people the impression that the casino is too loose with their comps.

- ❧ Ask if there are any packages that are out there for the dates that you want to stay.

- ❧ Never accept the central reservation number's first price. Always ask if there's something less. Central reservation is trained at profit making, so they'll start with their highest rate — but they'll do what it takes to earn your business. There's usually a low back up rate that they can sell to, and they get paid on commission, so they won't give up too easily.

🍸 Classic Vegas Mistake

Party Off: A lot of guys use having a room party as one of their primary motivating factors for upgrading to a suite. Although there are plenty of great reasons to upgrade to a suite, having a room party ain't one of them. This is not Boise, this is Vegas. What can you do in your room that you can't do anywhere else in town? There's always an open bar, so saying it's the only place for a nightcap is not much of an excuse. It's one thing to convince some women to come back up to your room to call it a night; it's another to actually plan a party in your room. If you opt to plan a party in your room, expect that you and your friends will be the only ones attending. And if things get out of hand, you'll have to live with the consequences. Even in the largest suites you might need to sleep in close quarters, so why ruin your good time by having to sleep in a bed that got soaked with beer — or worse — during your lame party?

♣ Even if you find yourself at the front desk without a room, call the central reservation number from your cell phone. The front desk will only offer the highest price possible.

Book a Suite

When it comes to booking your room, a suite is probably the best option. A suite will allow you to fit more guys into one space in style. A suite serves as a meeting place for your group, a place to hang while everyone is still getting ready. It's much nicer to sit on a couch and catch a little Sports Center than on the end of a bed. You only live once, so buck up, you cheap bastard, and get a suite! Just remember that there are so many different types of them, you'll quickly learn that in Vegas, "suite" is a relative term.

Types of Suites

There are several different grades of suites. Although every hotel uses different naming conventions, their suites all fall into the following four categories.

Executive or Petite Suites

Slightly bigger than a standard hotel room, these suite types feature a couch, coffee table and sitting area that is part of the room. Some hotels such as the Rio, the Venetian, and THEhotel are all this level of room, and bill themselves as being an "all suite" establishment. However, make no mistake: If you're looking for a major suite this won't live up to your expectations.

Examples of this grade are: TI, Caesars petite suites, and Rio's standard suite. Sleeps: 3. Pushing It: 4.

One-Bedroom Suites

This level of suite features a separate living room that has a sitting area. The bedroom is separate from the sitting room. Essentially, a one-bedroom apartment.

Examples of this grade are: MGM's Hollywood suite and Hard Rock's Deluxe suite. Sleeps: 4. Pushing It: 5.

Two-Bedroom Suites

A separate living room with two adjoining king-size bed bedrooms. The living room usually features a bar and a dining table.

Examples of this grade are: Flamingo's luxury suite, TI's Penthouse suite and MGM's Marquis suite. Sleeps: 5. Pushing It: 8 (with rollaways).

Rain Man Suites

Unfortunately, Trent and Mike never did get the keys to one of these palatial pads in Swingers. This level of suite refers to any suite that goes above and beyond the two-bedroom suites. These suites are usually reserved for the casino high rollers, making them tough to rent. Usually the two-bedroom suite is the most they'll offer you. Although these accommodations are really impressive, you came to Vegas to have fun, not sit around in the room all day with a bunch of guys. So don't sulk over the fact that these rooms are off-limits. Besides, when they are available to reserve, they're a small fortune. Examples of this grade are: Hard Rock's Penthouse suite and Caesars' Duplex suite. Sleeps: 8. Pushing It: 20 (using every square inch).

☂ Classic Vegas Mistake

Up Close and Personal: As if you needed another reason to buck up for a suite, there's always this: If you are here for a bachelor party and hire a stripper to entertain you in your room, there's nothing more pathetic than watching her in a standard room. You'll be crammed onto a queen-size bed with your friends, and the 500-pound guy who escorts her can hardly fit through the door — it's just not pretty.

Note: Most suites come with king-size beds. It is very rare to find a suite that has two beds, so be sure to ask about the number of beds when you are booking. For the executive and one-bedroom suites, book the connecting room, since it usually has two double or queen beds.

PUT YOUR HOTEL TO WORK

You've chosen your hotel, now it's time to put it to work. Here's how to get the most out of your hotel. Let it work for you.

Your Grand Arrival

The Hotel Entrance
Make sure you arrive at the right door. Hotels have many different entrances, and there is nothing worse than having a taxi driver drop you off at an entrance only to have to bring your bags through the casino to find hotel registration. Always specify that you want to be dropped off at the hotel entrance.

Carry Your Bags
If you followed the *Little Black Book's* advice, you'll only have a carry on bag that you can bring to the room yourself. Getting your bags sent up to the room can take forever, especially if you're checking in on a Friday. Save yourself the time and skip the bell service.

The Side Valet
Most hotels have a side valet. They're at the side and allow you to enter and exit with greater ease. You'll get your car a lot quicker if you park with these guys than if you park with the main valet.

What to Remember at Check-In

❀ If it's an option, you might want to check in at the airport. Some hotels offer this service, and it's a great way to avoid what can be a huge line once you get to your hotel. Let them give you your keys and take your bags, while you head off to get your adventure started. It is an easy way to add an extra hour to your fun.

❀ Always ask how much for a suite upgrade. If is it around $40 or less, then go for it. Just make sure that you know what type of suite you are being upgraded to. You don't want to pay extra for a glorified standard room.

❀ Dress nice and look important when you check in. If you look like a scrub, then the hotel's front desk agent may put you in a second-tier room. As with most things in life, good-looking people get all the breaks.

❀ Just send one guy to check-in. If you overwhelm the clerk they'll happily put you in a room right next to the laundry facilities or the room service kitchen.

❀ Ask for a room key for each guy in the group. There's nothing worse than being locked out of your room at 5 a.m. because your buddy inside is passed out and can't hear you banging on the door and leaving voice mails on his cell phone.

❀ Make sure to ask if there is a "fun book" for guests. These books have coupons in them for free table bets and discounted food.

Tip Well at Check-In

Flashing a tip to the person at the registration desk can pay off. Here are a few things you want to ask if they can do for you.

♣ Ask to be put in the new tower. This is Vegas: Every place has a new tower, and at a property like Caesars Palace, the difference between the new and the old tower is night and day. The rooms in the old tower are always smaller — they're products of the old days, when they didn't want you to be so comfortable in your room that you'd not be out on the floor gambling.

♣ Ask to be near the elevator. If you aren't, you'll regret it. Remember, we're talking about the largest hotels on earth; walking from the elevator to your room can often be confusing, tedious and tiring.

♣ Ask for either a Strip view or pool view. If you spend more than five minutes in your room (and despite your best intentions, you will be in your room for more than five minutes), you'll want to have something to look at. You didn't fly all the way out Vegas just to stare at a giant air-conditioning unit or a banquet facility, did you? Although less desirable than the Strip view, the pool view is practical since you can look down in the morning to see if it's too crowded to head down for some poolside action.

♣ Standard rooms. Many hotels have different sizes of standard rooms. If you don't get the suite upgrade, ask for the largest standard available.

Charge It: Get on the Property's Radar

Hotels are starting to look at the overall value of the guest — not only on gaming, but also on hotel room rate, food, spa, show and gift shop expenditures. If you have high expenses, you may be getting offers in the mail from them to come back.

Make sure you charge every on-property expense to your room. This way, you'll get credit for what you spend. Just make sure your friends pony up when the bill comes around. Your friends would never stiff you, would they?

Remember Me: Get the Concierge on Your Side

The best friend an unprepared traveler can have is an attentive concierge. A good concierge can put you in the heart of the action. They have a fairly elaborate network of access to restaurants, clubs, shows, and events.

Even though you might have made every effort possible to plan ahead, perhaps there's a thing or two you overlooked. Or perhaps you got everything you wanted, just not when you wanted it. Well, the concierge might be able to help.

What to Do

When you check in, go over to the concierge's desk, introduce yourself, and slip him/her $50 dollars. Say, "Keep me on top of things." This way, he or she will have you in mind if something comes up.

What You Can Expect

If you have a reservation at the right restaurant at the wrong time, ask if he can help you out. If you're looking for tickets to a show at the last minute, give him a ring. Don't count on him having a dozen tickets to O on hand, but he will be able to get you some options. You are paying for the inside track and if you've got questions, he's got answers. If you think $50 is a lot to part with, think again. That $50 can be the difference between an okay meal at a ho-hum restaurant and a table at a place that would have required weeks of advance notice to make a reservation. He also can get you a rental car at the hotel so you don't have to take a shuttle to the car rental place or pay the airport tax fee. You came all the way out here, and you only get a couple of nights out with the guys, aren't you worth it?

Need a Drink? Stock Up or Pay Up

In the old days there were never minibars in rooms. Why? Because management wanted to get you out of your room and onto the gaming floor if you wanted a drink. Although drinks are generally cheap or "free" in Las Vegas, the minibar's still no bargain. There are plenty of cheap liquor stores on the Strip, so pick up a bottle and some mixers and bring them back with you. Most properties are starting to sell small bottles in their sundries store, so make a purchase before you head up to your room.

If you really need a drink and didn't stop for a bottle, go ahead and bust in to the minibar: You flew all the way out here, and you're going to go cheap when you really need a little pick-me-up? Just remember, that Heineken just cost you half a lap dance.

🍸 Classic Vegas Mistake

The Double Tip: A limo driver drops off a group of guys, the first guy out of the limo tips the driver a $20. Seconds later, another guy tips him another $20. The limo driver is not going to say a thing, but he just got double tipped. This happens all the time. A limo driver once told us that four guys out of a group of eight tipped him. They each thought they were the only one tipping. When you are with a large group of guys, discuss before the money starts exchanging hands who is going to tip.

Checking Out

When you check out, don't waste your time standing in the long line at the front desk. Use the check-out on your television, or just leave and have the bill put on your credit card.

Check-out times are not set in stone. If they say check-out time is 10 a.m. don't worry if is it 11a.m. before you check out. If they call your room, just tell them you are packing up your stuff.

If your flight leaves later, check your bags in with the bellboy. If you are going to spend the rest of your time at a different hotel before you leave, bring your bags with you and check them with the bell desk at that hotel. You don't have to be a guest at a facility to check your bags.

 ## Roughing It: Doing Vegas with No Hotel Room

❀ Make sure you have a car because you can always crash in it. If you have no hotel and no car, you will be hurting for certain.

❀ Don't stay out too late, because you won't be able to sleep when the sun is out. Don't get too drunk, either. You will need to be able to drive from one parking spot to another if security finds you sleeping in the car.

❀ Park someplace where you won't be blinded by the morning sun. Big parking garages such as at the MGM Grand and Rio are good places. Park away from where people will walk past your car to get to the casino.

❀ Sleep in the backseat. In the front seat, you will be spotted quicker by security and they will kick you out.

❀ Crack your window a little bit so the moisture does not build up.

❀ When you wake up, change your clothes in the car, put some deodorant on, and head into the casino. You will be greasy at this point, so dip your head in the sink and freshen up. Wear a hat to hide your hair, and then pop in a breath mint.

Chapter 5

Dining:
A Man's Gotta Eat

When it comes to eating in Las Vegas, you've got lots of options. Sometimes it can seem as if there are too many. We've seen guys wander up and down the Strip unable to make up their mind, looking for the right place to eat, only to settle on a hot dog as their only option other than passing out. It's important to have a game plan, to know that not every meal needs to be memorable, and that sometimes you just need to chow down and keep partying on. On the other hand, Las Vegas is chock-full of fine dining. For those looking to eat well, it's a gourmand's delight.

 STANDARD CASINO RESTAURANTS

In addition to the 24-hour coffee shop covered in Chapter 4, every casino has several different restaurants. These are the standard types:

❀ The buffet: A true Las Vegas classic, the buffet is a massive restaurant designed to bring in the masses. The buffets are a loss leader, used to draw more people into the casino.

❀ The steak house: The gourmet room of the casino. The steak house features, well . . . steak, as well as chicken and seafood presented in a refined manner.

❧ The ethnic restaurant: Chinese, Italian, Mexican, and Japanese establishments add a touch of diversity to the casino, as the other restaurants feature red, white, and blue fare.

❧ The snack shop: Sometimes referred to as the sandwich shop, this walk up eatery is usually located near the sportsbook.

> ## 🍸 Classic Vegas Mistake
>
> **The Group Wander:** Don't just wander around in a group looking for a place to eat. Every day we see groups that just keep walking around, their blood sugar dropping, looking for relief, and no one knowing what the others want to eat. They end up tired and pissed at one another. Instead, grab a seat at your command central, the casino center bar, and use the *Little Black Book* to facilitate a discussion on where to eat. If your friends aren't up for a discussion, hit the closest place we recommend.

The Buffet

The buffet is a legend of the Las Vegas Strip. Vegas casinos have made an art of the chow line. Every group of guys needs to pay homage to this festival of food options: It's a Vegas tradition. Pick a good one, pay your entry fee, and go to town. If you do it right, one meal at the buffet is about all your group will be able to take.

Why Buffets Are Great for Guys

❧ Shorter meal time. The line might be long and the wait twenty minutes, but remember when you get in, you get to eat immediately. This is often quicker than the coffee shop affair.

❧ Something for everybody. With so many food choices and the blood sugar getting low in your group, the buffet will have something that everyone in your group will find appetizing.

❀ It's loud. You can be loud, drunk, or hung over. Your drunken friends won't embarrass you as they will in a coffee shop or steak house. Most of the time you will be stuffing yourself with food so you won't have time for talking anyway.

❀ It's cheaper than you think. It might be a pretty penny to get in to the buffet, but your drinks are free and you only have to leave $1 tip per person.

Keys to a Good Buffet:

❀ Short wait. There is always a line at a buffet, but a good one moves.

❀ Quality food stations with attentive staff. Many buffets boast about their different types of food and desserts, but you should be concerned about quality rather than quantity. Who cares if they are amazing you with their chocolate sundae fountain display? Salads, desserts, soups, and breads are of no use to you. No one likes to stand around waiting for the food trays to refresh. It's important to find a place that stays on top of getting the trays swapped out, otherwise you're likely to settle on some food you don't want just for the sake of getting something. A good buffet has solid offerings in meats, seafood, Asian, Italian, Mexican, and Mongolian stations.

❀ Relaxed atmosphere and clean facility. The buffet is an endless round of people chowing down; its job is to get as many people in and out of there as fast as possible, so sometimes they aren't able to keep up a clean facility, as the cleanup crew can't keep up with the spills. There is nothing worse than a grimy buffet. The atmosphere needs to allow for movement. You need to be able to get from one side to the other without fighting in the line with a family from Iowa.

❖ Reasonable pricing. Over the last couple of years, buffet prices have sky rocketed, and some just aren't worth it.

Black Book *Recommendations*

❖ `Dishes at TI. A great lunch or early dinner buffet, eat here before the Siren's Pirate show gets out. After the show, people flock into the casino and head straight to the buffet.

❖ Cravings at Mirage. The line looks long, but it moves fast. The Asian menu here is the tops. Ask for a table in the back; it is much closer to the good food, so you won't have to walk as much between courses.

❖ The Buffet at Mandalay Bay: Although it's not much to look at, the short lines, good food choices, and a coffee shop-type environment make The Buffet a good choice. You don't even feel you are at the buffet here.

❖ Luxor: The buffet is down the escalator near the sports-book. If the line is long, you should probably pass. Although the food is good, they're not great at moving people in and out of this place, so sometimes the coffee shop is a better option.

❖ Rio: Although it used to be ranked number one in Vegas, it seems to be fading some. Stick with the normal buffet near Bikini's and avoid the seafood buffet over in the Masquerade Village. This buffet is extremely popular, so go here at non-peak eating hours.

Hit the Buffet for Breakfast: Why It Beats the Coffee Shop

The buffet is often your best choice for breakfast. It usually has a short line and a low price, plus it has all the offerings of the coffee shop. The coffee shop and buffet often share the same kitchen, so the food quality at the coffee shop won't be much better. Plus, you can get a made-to-order omelet much faster than in the coffee shop.

Watch yourself. Don't fall into the buffet trap and go hog wild, loading your plate up with cheese blintzes and five pieces of chocolate chip French toast. Get what you would normally get in a coffee shop for breakfast; don't stray for the not so traditional breakfast items.

ⵗ◉ⵗ Room Service: A Great Breakfast Alternative

A great way to get your day going is having breakfast brought up to your room. You can sip a cup of coffee and have French toast while you are still waking up and getting ready. Sometimes it takes a while, so it makes sense to order the breakfast right before you go to sleep, either by calling down, or filling out the breakfast order card and hanging in on your doorknob. Then it will be there at the exact time you want it.

Save yourself the frustration of rousting everyone out of bed and getting them showered at the same time just so you can get some food. Otherwise, be prepared to wait forty-five minutes until everyone is ready to roll. Once you get everyone into the elevator, expect that they'll spend twenty minutes heading from place to place until they finally arrive on where they want to eat, then you'll need to get seated, order . . . you catch the drift. Fill out the breakfast card, hang it on your doorknob, and go to sleep.

You Versus The Buffet: A Title Card Bout

Although it's a fight that's seldom won, guys try all the time to beat the buffet by getting more than their money's worth. Remember that scene from the movie *Diner*, where the guy works his way through the whole left side of the menu? Surely at least one of the guys in your group wants to take down the buffet, perhaps in a futile attempt to get back the money he lost at the blackjack table. We've seen a lot of guys try and fail, but if you want to have a fighting chance, here's a strategy that works.

❧ Avoid the bread section.

Yes, management puts bread at the front on the buffet line so you'll fill up your plate and stomach with heavy, carbo-loaded bread.

❀ Avoid the salad section.

A selection of four different lettuces, ten different pasta salads, and cucumbers is just a low-cost gimmick. The casino isn't spending big bucks here, so pass.

❀ Avoid the soup.

You are at a buffet with a thousand other people opening up huge vats of soup. Trust us, the soup sucks.

❀ Stop 1: Seafood

Grab two plates to start at the seafood station. This is the most expensive part of the buffet, so stick it to them early. Load one plate up with peel-and-eat shrimp, the other with crab legs. Go back to your table and go to town on the light seafood. Avoid the butter and tarter sauce (don't let these rich temptations coat your tummy), and stick with the cocktail sauce.

❀ Stop 2: The Carving Station

Get a slice each of prime rib, pork roast, salmon, and turkey. Don't feel bad about making the carver work by switching pieces of meat, and don't accept his first serving — tell him to load your plate up. Back at the table, eat half of each meat and head back to the buffet. Sure, you didn't eat it all, but they had to pay for it.

❀ Stop 3: Chinese

This cuisine is known for never making you too full. Toss some sweet-and-sour chicken, pot stickers, crab Rangoon and pork rolls on your plate. Add a layer of fried rice on top with a serving of hot sauce and soy sauce.

✿ Stop 4: Mexican

Mexican usually consists of enchiladas, beans and rice, a make-your-own taco station (probably with no taco shells left), and a salsa station that looks like it has been hit by a tornado. Avoid this section altogether unless they have cheese quesadillas. These savory hand-size bites are great to top off your plate, but everything else is a pass.

✿ Stop 5: American

If they have baby back ribs, then load up. If not, check out the fried chicken. If you can find a breast (buffets are notorious for putting out only dark meat), then grab a piece. Don't weigh yourself down with mashed potatoes and gravy — they're just cheap filler.

✿ Stop 6: Mongolian BBQ

Pretty much every buffet has a Mongolian BBQ section. At this point you'll need a breather, so waiting a few minutes for the BBQ to cook is a good thing. Build a bowl of vegetables and ask for Mongolian chicken.

✿ Stop 7: Italian

Each buffet has an Italian section; stay away from the stuffed shells and only get the made-to-order pasta from the chef. A marinara sauce is a better choice than an Alfredo sauce at this point.

✿ Stop 8: Dessert

Take one plate and load up three of the smaller plates of different cakes and pies. Go back to your table and take a bite of each. Order a cup of coffee from the waitress and head back to dessert section for a build-your-own soft-serve sundae. Load up the sprinkles, chopped nuts, caramel and strawberries. Head back to the table and take your sweet-ass time drinking your coffee and eating your sundae.

You did it — you kicked the buffet's ass! You took 'em for all they had. They didn't even see what hit 'em. Now, maybe you should sit down and rest a bit.

> ## ☂ Classic Vegas Mistake
>
> Eating off the Strip: Although many of Vegas's restaurants are not located in casinos, not many are worth the time and money to travel to (there are a few exceptions; we recommend one, below). It might be easy to get a cab to take you there, but getting one to pick you again later can take up to an hour. Perhaps you'll want to head downtown for a meal, but that's really about it. You have every food option you can think of on, or adjacent to, the Strip.

The Steak house

The steak house is the only choice for the man's dinner. If you are out with the guys, avoid the chi-chi ethnic restaurants and head out for a real man's dinner: steak. While there are a lot of options not all are great for a group of guys, so here's what you need to consider.

Keys to a Good Steak house:

❀ Old-school steak house décor. A place with red leather booths and dim lighting is just what the doctor ordered.

❀ Prime, dry-aged beef. Beef is the only thing you should be eating at a steak house, so make sure they've got the good stuff. Cuts of beef are classified by the FDA grading system as commercial, select, choice or prime. Prime beef is the highest quality, having the best texture, firmness, color, and marbling. Dry-aging is a climate-controlled process of storing the beef under precise conditions of temperature, humidity, and air circulation to ensure the best tenderness and flavor. Ask you server about grades and aging before you order.

✸ Large-group seating. Not all places are designed to accommodate large groups; don't settle for makeshift seating arrangements or having to break your crew up into two groups. When you call ahead to book (always, always do this), check it out to make sure they fit your group in properly.

Black Book *Recommendations*

✸ The Steakhouse at Circus Circus: Circus Circus? Are you kidding me? Trust us, you'll be surprised at what you find. The Steakhouse at Circus Circus is a great old-school Vegas steak house. Your guys will feel right at home in their big leather booths. Adding to the décor, the steaks are cooked on an open charcoal pit in the middle of the room. The Steakhouse is in the back of the building, so have the cabbie drop you off at hotel check-in, not the front of the building. Otherwise, you'll have to wade through a sea of screaming kids and their gambling parents before you reach the restaurant.

✸ Hugo's Cellar at Four Queens: Four Queens, are you kidding me? Head to the back of the casino and proceed down the stairs into the dark dungeon. This place is so dark, you can barely see your food. The staff is great, and the food is even better.

✸ Piero's: Even though we're talking steak houses, you gotta put this place on your hit list. Although technically an Italian eatery, the filet is fantastic and it's so old-school-mobster Vegas, you'll be checking the door every time it opens expecting to see Bugsy Siegel walk through it.

✸ Smith & Wollensky: The Las Vegas location is across from the Monte Carlo. Be sure to go to the restaurant, not the café part; they're almost two different restaurants. If you have a big group be sure to reserve a private room.

❧ The Capital Grill at the Fashion Show Mall: Across from the Wynn, this is not the easiest place to get a reservation. If you show up without one, hit the bar. The bar and the bartenders are great, so grab a drink and a cigar. The filet here is a great choice.

❧ Lawry's The Prime Rib: The ultimate dining experience — if your group is four or fewer. Big groups are placed at large tables in the middle of the large, loud room. Good luck trying to carry on a conversation. The entire dining experience here is top-notch. The only thing to order is the prime rib, which will probably be the best you'll ever have. This is an exception to our rule about not eating off the Strip: It's a bit of a haul, so you may want to grab a rental car to get here or come here on the night you have a limo. The cab line is usually long, and the cabs are in short supply.

The "Strip" Steak: A Dining Adventure

If you're looking for something really unique try dinner at Treasures. Treasures is one of the few gentlemen's clubs with a real dining room. The menu at Treasures features excellent steak and seafood options. This isn't some lame attempt by a strip club to offer food — this is a true dining experience. The room décor, atmosphere, and food are first-rate. It makes for a fun evening to have dinner, then head into the club. You are separate from the club, but dancers stroll by your table checking up on you. Since you are eating they are not pressuring you to buy a dance; they're relaxed and cordial. This dinner will make for a good story with the guys back home. If you call ahead, they can send a car to pick you up.

How to Eat at a Vegas Steak house in 10 Easy Steps

Here's what you and the guys need to do to have a memorable dinner out on the town without breaking the bank.

1. Order a Gin Martini

Arrive a little early so you have time to head to the bar and order a stiff gin martini with three olives. This classic will take you back to old-school Vegas while you get ready for your meal.

2. Order Cheap Red Wine

You're probably already a little drunk anyway, so you probably won't be able to appreciate good wine — not that you'd be able to even if you were sober. Order a bottle of the cheapest red wine on the menu. Does it really matter if it's merlot, cabernet or pinot noir? Even if you do know the difference, we're sure your friends probably won't be impressed.

3. Avoid the Bottled Water

Stick with the tap water, pass on the still and sparkling.

4. Chow Down on the Bread.

The bread is excellent and free at steak houses. So order up, slather on some butter, and enjoy with your wine.

5. Pass on the Appetizers

You'll be tempted to order a couple of appetizers for the table to share. It's not easy to split most appetizers among more than four, usually someone is left out. On top of that, it is a pain to pass dishes around the table.

6. Avoid the Caesar Salad

Get a salad — just avoid the Caesar. Although it might be tasty, the Caesar is usually comprised of large leafs of uncut lettuce, making them a real pain in the neck to eat, and you'll feel like you're gardening. And, seeing that you have a couple in you, you might get a little careless with your utensils and wind up sending your fork flying.

7. Order Your Steak

Stick with the rib eye, medium. Real steak connoisseurs know that the rib eye is the choicest cut of meat. Don't even think about anything else. Filet, porterhouse, New York strip all take a backseat to the rib eye.

8. Order Your Sides

With only a couple of exceptions, most of these places are strictly a la carte. Choose one green, one potato, and one fungus. Sides at steak houses are meant to be split, so order one green side of asparagus or broccoli, one dish of mashed potatoes or hash browns and an order of sautéed mushrooms for the table.

9. Get a Cigar

Nothing is more satisfying than a nice fat cigar after a nice fat steak. Move your group into the bar and buy one in the $7 to $10 range. Sit back and relax.

10. The After Dinner Drink

The perfect complement to your cigar is a shot of Sambuca with espresso coffee beans, a good VSOP or XO cognac, or a single-malt scotch. Port is also traditional, but a bit heavy. Any of these are just what you need to get pumped up before you head out on the town. A note about single malts: This is not your dad's Cutty Sark, and if you order it on the rocks, the bartender will look at you like you deserve to be shot. And you do.

The Ethnic Restaurant

Various ethnic restaurants round out your dining options and offer a little variety.

Keys to a Good Ethnic Restaurant:

❧ Hip, hangout atmosphere with the possibility of meeting women

❧ Serves lunch and dinner

❧ Good food

Black Book *Recommendations*

❧ Isla at TI (New Age Mexican): Isla's not your standard Mexican restaurant. They feature a roving guacamole cart and a "Tequila Goddess" (a hot, costumed gal who dispenses the high-end tequilas).

❧ Okada at Wynn (Sushi): Not only is the sushi incredible here, but it is also a hip joint with a huge bar on the right and views of the Wynn waterfall in the back. It is located on top of Wynn's nightclub, so groups of girls eat here before they go out.

❧ Gonzalez and Gonzalez at New York–New York (Mexican):

Located in the street section of New York–New York, this is a fun place to get some traditional Mexican eats and margaritas. Sit in the inside section; the outside section's tables are right on top of each other. Keep an eye on the bar; a lot of women sit there for a little while to get margaritas to go.

❁ Mesa Grill at Caesars (Southwestern fusion): A favorite of women, you will see some real lookers here. Avoid sitting at the bar; it is right in the walkway and a bit uncomfortable.

❁ Simon's at Hard Rock (American): American is ethnic? In this case, yes. The menu here is a throwback to home cooking back when you were a kid. Stick with mom's favorites here like the meatloaf and macaroni & cheese. For desert the homemade Twinkies hit the spot. The bar here can be a great place to get away from the casino and have a drink. As a bonus, there are usually some hotties around.

❁ Pink Taco at Hard Rock (Mexican): A different type of Mexican food here. Try to eat at the bar or at a table around the bar, instead of getting a table. Stick with the simple stuff, like the fish tacos. Between that and chips you should have a solid base to drink a bunch of Coronas and talk to some ladies.

 Dinner Roulette

Want to make your meal a little more memorable? If you're dining at a casino restaurant, collect from your friends for the bill, then place a bet at a roulette table. Have everyone wait at the table while one of you puts the cash on red or black. If you lose, you overpay for your meal; if you win everyone's happy. This is a great way to have some fun with everyone. How often do you all get to place one bet together with immediate results? It sure beats the old "credit card roulette" game where you all throw your cards in, the waitress picks one at random, and that guy gets stuck with the bill.

The Snack Shop

When someone in the group is hungry or you have only a little time on your hands and you would rather spend it gambling, snack shops are perfect. It's also a spot to grab a quick bite if you are waiting around for someone.

A Good Snack Shop Should:

✿ Offer enough choices (some places are glorified hot dog stands)

✿ Prepare the food fresh; you are not at a 7-11 getting pre-made sandwiches

✿ Be quick to get in and get out

✿ Offer table seating. You need somewhere to eat so you don't have to stand in the back of the sportsbook eating your sandwich

Black Book *Recommendations*

✿ Canter's Deli at TI: Near the entrance of Tangerine, this New York Deli gives you huge deli sandwiches. Order the sandwiches that make New York delis famous, the Reuben or the pastrami on rye.

✿ Snacks at Bellagio: Between the Sports book and the restaurant FIX, Snacks offers gourmet snacks served quickly. Stick with menu items such as the corn chowder served in a bread bowl.

✿ Toscano's Deli at the Rio: On the left side of the sportsbook, Toscano's will hit the spot with a selection of grilled sandwiches such as the Philly cheese steak.

The Snack Shop Is the Only Place to Eat on Arrival

By the time they get checked into their hotel, most guys we know are usually hungry. Well, your first night in Vegas you should be concentrating on partying, not eating. You're finally here, you have to hit the Strip hard, so pass on the sit-down meal and hit the snack shop. It will fill your stomach and not take too much away from your drinking.

★ Three More Coffee Shops That Don't Suck ★

Looking for more 24-hour options? Give these a try.

The Bellagio Café:
Nestled in the corner of the Bellagio conservatory, Bellagio goes over the top with their 24-hour coffee shop. The wait in line is pretty quick, if you go in the mornings grab a cup of complimentary gourmet coffee as you wait. Ask for a seat on the right-hand side so you have the ambience of the conservatory flowers. This café also has smoking hot keno runners. Play a couple dollars as you wait for your food. The top menu item is the chicken penne pasta.

The Grand Lux Café at the Venetian:
Managed by the Cheesecake Factory group, the Grand Lux is a great dining experience. If the wait is too long, head to the bar area where there's usually a highboy table to sit at. If you do get seated ask for a table on the patio, so you can people-watch the girls coming down the escalator into the casino.

The Peppermill:
If you are on the north part of the Strip and have a rental car, the Peppermill is a great coffee shop choice. This old-school Vegas favorite has something for everyone. The best menu choices are breakfast items.

THE BIG MEAL

The big meal is the signature meal of the guy's weekend. It's when everyone gets dressed up and ready to throw down the meal of all meals. This is the one meal you should be ready to buck up for. It's one of the biggest events of your weekend and it's a meal you're going to remember for years to come, so don't screw it up.

🍸 Classic Vegas Mistake

High and Dry: If you have a large group of guys who want the big meal, do your homework before you go to Vegas. Large group seating is hard to find, and the reservations are booked weeks in advance. If you don't, your group will be stuck in the middle of a loud dining room with tables pushed together and everyone sitting on top of one another. And, for what you're going to be paying, everyone will agree this is not the experience you are looking for. Reservations are free — make some.

When to Do the Big Meal

The big meal should be on day two of the guy's weekend. On day one, everyone is still arriving and all jazzed up about being in Vegas. Day two, everyone is a little bit cooler and nobody is worried about filling up their stomach too much before going out.

Where to Do the Big Meal

Not all steak houses are good for the big meal. Some steak houses can accommodate large groups, others cannot. Get buy-in from everyone and do your research; otherwise you'll regret it.

Steak houses that can take big groups:
- Smith & Wollensky, across from Monte Carlo. Your choice of three separate rooms, one being the "kitchen table," which is a glass-enclosed table overlooking the kitchen.

* Capital Grill, inside the Fashion Show Mall. The bigger tables are located near the windows with spectacular views of the strip.

* Foundation Room at Mandalay Bay. With stunning views of the Strip, this restaurant features large, private rooms for cocktails and dinner.

* Del Frisco's, off the Strip near the Hard Rock. A short cab ride off the Strip, Del Frisco's has many private rooms to host groups of all sizes, including a huge cigar-smoking lounge for the post dinner stogie.

* Okada at Wynn Las Vegas. The only restaurant for the big meal that is not a steak house, this high-end sushi restaurant features private rooms for eight that over look the Wynn waterfall.

* Austin's at Texas Station. Although located about 15 minutes off the Strip, Austin's is the top-ranked steak house in town. The private dining room with a large, round table along with the impeccable service makes Austin's worth mentioning.

The Preset Menu – A Smart Choice

Many steak houses offer the set menu for a large group of people. These menus have prearranged pricing, so it does not feel like a competition between everyone. Some even have a price for un-limited amount of drinks for a certain time period.

Cigars – Make the Meal a Celebration

It's great to get together with your whole group, light up cigars, and shoot the shit. You can always avoid the expense and limited selection at the restaurant by bringing your own. In addition to the cigar boutiques inside most major hotels, there are a number

$$$ IF MONEY IS NO OBJECT

Let the Server Order for You: Don't even look at the menu. Tell the server that money is no object and you want a grand meal prepared by the head chef. The server and chef will be honored by your trust in them and they will prepare a magnificent meal specifically for you. Each course will be a delectable surprise and, at the end, the chef will personally come out to meet you.

of small liquor stores on the Strip that carry a good selection of cigars. Distribute a cigar to everyone in our group and smoke them together in celebration. Here are a few basics for making your selection.

Selecting a Cigar

❧ <u>Origin</u>. Stick with cigars from Honduras or the Dominican Republic. Other cigars from Jamaica, Brazil, Costa Rica, and Nicaragua are good only if you really know what you are doing.

❧ <u>Brand</u>. Choose from the following types: Padrón, Davidoff, Don Tomas, Montecristo, Macanudo, Avo, or Romeo y Julieta. All the lesser known brands can be hit-or-miss on quality.

❧ <u>Wrapper</u>. Select one with a lighter color wrapper. Cigars with dark wrappers have a much stronger taste that will be overwhelming for the novice.

❧ <u>Size.</u> Stick with smaller size Corona or Robusto, and avoid the big sizes of Presidentes, Double Coronas, and Churchill's. Sure, the huge cigars look cool, but they take literally forever to smoke.

What to Do Next

The big meal is going to fill you up big-time. You're not going to feel like going out; you will be a little worn down. Some of your guys are going to want to go back to the hotel and go to bed. You owe it to the group to keep things moving.

Have a plan for what to do afterward, otherwise you'll all end up going back to your hotel, having a drink or two, and will wind up watching the "players" in your group lose some money at the tables. This isn't our idea of a good time, and you shouldn't settle for letting this lame-o fate befall your crew. Perhaps a bar or gentlemen's club is your best bet. Whatever you choose, decide ahead and keep your boys moving.

> ### ☒ Classic Vegas Mistake
>
> **The Cuban Cigar:** Although smoking a Cuban cigar is a treat, the U.S. still prohibits importing cigars from Cuba. If someone (such as a bathroom attendant) is touting that they can sell you a Cuban, it is probably either a Cuban company — such as Cohiba — that has moved their operations to another country, or a normal cigar with a fake Cuban label. Don't pay the premium prices for a Cuban knockoff, because it is not the real thing.

Chapter 6

Gambling:
Letting It Ride in Sin City

*···

If you don't like to gamble, don't come to Las Vegas. There are plenty of things you can do here that you can't do anywhere else, but at the top of that list is gambling. Every other gambling town throughout the country — be it the shabby, geriatric-filled halls of Atlantic City, the cavernous Foxwoods, or the overcrowded riverboats of Illinois — is strictly junior varsity compared with Vegas. This town has them all beat, and we're sure you're ready to bring down the house. Fortunes are won and lost here every day; don't you want to be a part of that?

Plenty of books will offer you surefire systems on killing them at the tables, but we won't. We'll give you an overview of your best gambling options, a few mistakes to avoid, and how to play with the guys. It's really not a lot of fun to play when your friends are just staring over your shoulder. If you're going to do that, you might as well be at home in your boxers playing poker on the Internet. Spend your time playing games where everyone can have a good time.

♠ WHY YOU SHOULD GAMBLE ON THIS TRIP

Gambling is the top attraction in Vegas, but the guy's trip is not just about trying to beat the house. Here are a few reasons that most don't think about.

Playing with the Boys

Sure, you came to Vegas to try and win a few bucks, but you didn't come to do it alone. Gambling with the boys is something you have to do. Throwing back some drinks, winning a few hands, and losing a few hands with your friends is what the guy's trip to Vegas is all about.

Meeting Women

While it is tough to pick up a woman while playing, certain games such as roulette and pai gow poker offer opportunities to chat it up and have a good time with the ladies. You won't meet any women just walking around the casino, so the games offer you a chance to make small talk between hands. If you at least introduce yourself to her while you are playing, perhaps you can throw out a good line or two if you bump into her later in the evening. Everyone is pretty open when they're winning, so take advantage of that fact and make some new friends.

Storytelling

You need to come back from Vegas with a gambling story or two. It's basically required that you play just so you can answer the question "How did you do?" Nobody wants the answer to be, "I didn't gamble at all." If that's all you have to say, don't be surprised to hear, "Then what'd you go to Vegas for?" Gambling can be a huge rush, and more often a huge heartbreak. Within that drama rests some great stories waiting to be told. We're not saying you should bet the farm, but you should at least put a few bucks into play. Otherwise, what did you go to Vegas for?

What to Play

There are many ways to lose your money in the casino. You'll stumble across all sorts of strange games, including some will make you just scratch your head such as War (that's right, you can bet on the kid's card game War). Stick with these classics:

Blackjack

This is the most popular game in the casino. It's a simple game that anyone can learn, and everyone enjoys. If you're playing at the right time of day, your friends can grab a seat beside you for a few hands and together you'll run the table.

How to Play

Blackjack pits each player against the dealer. The object is to amass a total point value that is greater than the dealer's without going over twenty-one. Numbered cards are worth their face value (the nine of hearts is worth nine; the four is worth four, etc.), and face cards are all worth ten points. An ace may be played as either a one or an eleven. If the player's card total goes over twenty-one, the player "busts" and automatically loses, no matter what the dealer's total.

Each player is dealt two cards, face up. The dealer is dealt two cards, but one of them is dealt face down; this card is referred to as the "hole" card. If the player is dealt an ace and a face card, he has a "blackjack" and automatically wins and gets paid before the dealer plays. For any hand other than "blackjack," the player has options. The player can "hit" and ask for another card, or "stand" and not accept any more cards. If the player has two of the same-valued cards, the player can "split" the cards and play two separate hands. This requires another wager equal to the first wager. With any two cards, a player may also "double down," which is an additional bet that is up to the value of the original bet. The player then receives only one card and may not "hit" again.

Once all players at the table have played their hands, then the dealer plays. The dealer has a standard set of rules. If the dealer's total is sixteen or less, then the dealer must hit. If the dealer's total is seventeen or greater, then the dealer must stand. After the dealer plays, if the player's total is greater than the dealer's, then the player wins. If the hands are a tie, the game is declared a "push" and the original bet is returned to the player. If the dealer's total is greater than the player's, then the player loses.

Tips on Playing

1. <u>Assume the Dealer's Hole Card is a Ten</u>: There are more tens than any other card in the deck, so always assume the hole card is a ten. If the dealer's up card is a two, three, four, five, or six, then assume the dealer has to hit and therefore has a good change of busting. If the dealer's up card is a seven, eight, nine, ten, face card or Ace, then assume the dealer has a good hand and will stand (if the dealer's up card is an ace and hole card is a face card, the dealer automatically has blackjack, and wins.)

2. <u>Play Your Hand Based on the Dealer's Face Card</u>: Play your hand based on what you think the dealer will (or must) do by the evidence of his up card. If the dealer has a two, three, four, five, or six showing, then hit when your total is eleven or less, and stand when your total is twelve or more. If the dealer has a seven, eight, nine, ten, face card or ace showing, then hit when your total is sixteen or less and stand when your total is seventeen or more.

3. <u>Doubling Down</u>: The simplest strategy is to always double on an eleven and double on a ten if the dealer has nine or less showing. There are more advanced options of doubling down on other numbers, but you will always be safe if you stick with the basics. .

4. <u>Splitting</u>: Always split when you have a pair of aces or

eights. Other splits can be slightly beneficial with certain cards, but they are not that simple to understand.

5. <u>Buy a Strategy Card</u>: A strategy card will show you the optimum play for every hand in blackjack. Once you know how to play every hand, it's just a matter of luck. Buy a strategy card at the hotel gift shop or download one from the Internet; it'll tell you everything you need to know.

6. <u>Learn the Game Mechanics</u>: The hand signals might seem simple, but many a player has looked like an idiot or, even worse, lost a lot of money simply because he didn't know the signals. To "hit," scratch your two fingers towards you on the table. To "stay," wave your hand once over the table. To "double down" or "split," place another bet alongside your current bet. The dealer will adjust the cards and continue.

7. <u>Start with the Shoe Games</u>: The shoe games are those that use four or six decks of cards, all shuffled together and dealt from a single feeder, or "shoe." They are simpler to play and think through than single or double deck games because all cards are out front, faceup on the table. It will be easier to keep track of everyone's hand (except, of course, for the dealer's). Once you have been playing for a while, then move on to the single and double deck games (discussed below) if you desire.

☗ Classic Vegas Mistake

Not Knowing How to Play: Nothing is worse than starting to play a game when you don't know how. If you are going to play a game that you have never played before, study the basic rules of the game before you start playing. If you don't, you are going to end up losing money learning how to play and embarrassing yourself at the table. There are plenty of books out there that will tell you everything you need to know.

---

8. <u>Don't Count Cards</u>: Don't confuse yourself on card counting systems. Card counting is very difficult and you will end up losing more hands if you don't do it right, or if you have had a couple of drinks and miss a card or two. The casinos frown on it anyway, and successful card counters eventually get banned from play. While that's assuredly not going to be you, you don't want to risk getting 86'd from the casino, do you?

9. <u>Sit in First or Second Base</u>: If you are new to gambling or your blackjack skills are a bit rusty, you want sit on the right-hand side of the table, preferably in the first base position that is dealt to first. This way, you won't be caught up with all the action of the other players, and if you make a bonehead move that causes all the players to lose, they won't be able to directly blame it on you because so many cards had been played since your move. In the third base position, you are last to be dealt to before the dealer. Make the wrong move and the dealer will get a different card than he would have had you played correctly, and everyone might lose. Do that enough and the other players will blame you for losing — not an experience you will really cherish.

10. <u>Avoid Insurance</u>: Insurance is a side bet that allows the player not to lose their original bet if the dealer has a blackjack. A player may only take insurance when the dealer is showing an ace. Trust us, this is a sucker's bet, as the odds are far in the casino's favor.

11. <u>Avoid Surrender</u>: Many casinos allow you to forfeit your hand without playing it for half of your bet. Although this is a minor part of basic strategy that improves your percentage on some hands, all the other guys at your table with think you are a girlie man and don't want to win. So, save face with the boys and don't surrender.

12. Avoid Side Bets: Many blackjack games have additional side bet games at the tables. Royal Match and Super 7s are examples, but forget 'em. The odds on these side games are terrible, and they're just trying to get you to bet more. Avoid the temptation and stick to the regular game.

13. Avoid "Feeling the Cards": Sometimes players ignore basic strategy and either hit or stand when they shouldn't because they have a "feeling" about the cards. Blackjack is math: It's a numbers game, and illogical play will change the natural flow of the cards. Your fellow players will not appreciate this when you, and they, lose.

Playing Single or Double Deck Blackjack

Single and double deck blackjack is dealt differently from the four or six deck shoe games. The cards are dealt facedown to each player, making it difficult to count cards. With single and double deck blackjack, the player picks up the cards and views them. This is a departure from the more common multi deck version where the player isn't allowed to touch the cards.

- If you want a hit, scratch the cards on the table.

- If you want to stand, stick the cards facedown underneath your chips in the betting circle.

- If you get a blackjack, immediately throw your cards face up to show the dealer.

- If you want to split or double down, throw your cards face up and make the additional wager

- If you bust out, throw your cards faceup onto the table.

If this is your first time playing single or double deck, be sure to watch the games for a couple minutes to get the motions down; if you don't, you might end up looking like an idiot.

Craps

Craps should be used to settle all differences in the world. You'll see the most culturally diverse groups of people celebrating together as they play. If they weren't playing craps, they could well be at one another's throats. This is *the* game to play with the boys: You're all winning and losing at the same time. Some of your best gambling stories will come from shooting craps.

How to Play

A craps game starts out when the pair dice are given to a new player, or "shooter". The shooter places a pass line wager and rolls the dice. The first roll of the dice is called the "come out roll". If the shooter rolls a seven or eleven, then the pass line wins and shooter rolls another come out roll. If the shooter rolls a two, three, or twelve, the pass line loses and the shooter again rolls another come out roll. If a four, five, six, nine or ten is rolled, then that number becomes "the point."

Once the point is established, the shooter keeps rolling until he rolls the point number or a seven. If the shooter rolls the point number, then the shooter "made the point" and the entire process repeats itself with the same shooter with another come out roll. If the shooter "sevens out," then the game is over and the dice move clockwise to the next shooter.

Bets to Make

❧ The Pass Line Bet. This bet is made before the come out roll by placing a bet on the pass line, which is on the outside of the table. You win even money on the bet when the shooter makes the point number. Always bet the table minimum on the pass line bet. If you wish to bet more, increase your odds bet or bet another type of bet.

❧ The Odds Bet: The odds bet is an even money bet that is placed behind your pass bet. The bet is made only after the point is established. This bet is a 0 percentage bet for the casino. The casino has no advantage when a player makes this bet. The bet wins when the shooter makes the point number. Most tables offer two times odds (2x), meaning that you can bet $10 on the odds bet if you have a $5 pass bet going. Some off-Strip Vegas casinos offer ten times and even hundred times odds. If you don't take the odds, you will look like a novice gambler, and the dealers and everyone at the table will keep telling you to make the odds bet.

❧ The Six and Eight Place Bets: Place bets are side bets on a number that you can put up and take down at any time. While you can bet four, five, six, eight, nine or ten, the only ones that you want to bet are the six or eight. These bets payouts are 7 : 6, so make sure you bet in increments of $6, or you won't get the full payout.

Tips on Playing

1. <u>Play at a Full Table:</u> Craps is a social game, and it's not nearly as much fun if there's no one to talk to. Plus, at a full table it takes a long time for the dealers to pay out all the bets, so you won't be playing as fast. You'll extend the life of your bankroll, chat up the choice ladies, and get your share of "free" cocktails.

2. <u>Don't Play the Don't Pass Bet</u>: This bet is the opposite of the pass line bet, except you are betting that a seven will be rolled before the shooter makes the point. Don't pass bettors really piss everyone off; some players are insulted because you are hoping the shooter will lose.

3. <u>Learn Dice Etiquette</u>: You don't want to look like a novice when handling the dice. First, pick up the dice with one hand instead of two. Next, don't bring the dice above the rim of the

table. Blowing on the dice is strictly for the movies — if you do it, you'll look like an idiot. Now, use an underhand motion and throw a nice soft arc having the dice first hit the table about three fourths down on the table. The dice should bounce once, and then bounce off the backstop of the table and come to a stop on the far side. Look, if you don't put enough mustard behind it, the dice will drop in the middle of the table and you'll get a reaction akin to that person who throws out the opening pitch only to have the ball hit the dirt fifteen feet in front of the catcher. Conversely, you don't want to put so much behind it that the dice ricochets off the table and onto the floor. If that happens, just quietly head for the door. Practice makes perfect, so pick up a pair of dice in the gift shop and throw them in your room. If you're still not comfortable with your throws, just let someone else be the shooter.

4. <u>Make Fun Bets While the Table Is Hot:</u> While the winning percentages are low, there are some bets that are just fun to do. The "hardways" are bets on the four, six, eight, or ten that the number will be hit with double dice before a seven, or the number with two other dice is hit. For example, a "hard four" bet is saying that "two and two" will be rolled before any combination of a seven or a "soft four" of a three and one. The "yo" bet is a one-roll bet where you win if an eleven is rolled. Only bet $1 on the yo bet. Get into it and yell it out like the rest of the players.

5. <u>Tip by Placing Bets for the Dealers</u>: The best way to tip is to place a bet for the dealers. Do this by throwing a $5 toward the stickman and yelling "Horn high yo for the boys." The "horn bet" is a one-roll $1 bet on the two, three, eleven, and twelve. The "high yo" means that the extra $1 from the $5 goes on the eleven, making the eleven a $2 bet. While most people don't know what it means, the dealers know and they will be excited. It's a good way to keep the energy up for the table.

Pai Gow Poker

Blackjack is not the only card game in town; switch it up with pai gow poker. With Pai gow poker, you can play for hours and barely lose any money because 60 percent of all hands end up in a tie between the dealer and the player. Pai gow poker is a great game for friends because you can show each other your cards and give advice on how to play. It's a slower game than blackjack, and is not a big money maker for the casino, so they don't put their top dealers on it. That means a slower pace of play, and thus, more "free" drinks and time to socialize with the ladies who seem to flock to this fun, unorthodox game.

How to Play

Pai gow poker is played like blackjack, where each player is playing against the dealer. The players and the dealer are each dealt seven cards. The player must then make two poker hands of cards, a five-card hand and a two-card hand. The five-card hand must be a better hand than the two-card hand. For example, if a player only has a pair of queens in the seven cards, then the pair must be kept in the five-card hand.

After the players have made their hands, the dealer also makes two hands and all the hands are revealed. To win, the player must win both hands. The player's five-card hand has to beat the dealer's five-card hand and the player's two-card hand has to beat the dealer's two-card hand. If the player loses one hand to the dealer, then the bet is a push. If the player loses both hands to the dealer, than the player loses the bet.

Tips on Playing

1. <u>Play the Hands According to the Rules</u>: Remember, the best value hand is played in the five-card hand; the two-card hand is the second value hand. If you get this wrong, your hand will automatically lose. Be sure to study up on the rules on pai gow poker before you play.

2. <u>Remember the Vig</u>: The Vig (short for "vigorish") is a percentage that the house takes out on each winning bet you have. If you don't have quarters and half dollars, they will keep a running total of the money you owe, and when you leave the table, you'll have to pay up. Don't leave the table with zero money or you might have to suffer the indignity of being escorted to the ATM machine by security. This *will* happen. They won't let it slide.

3. <u>Ask for Help</u>: Pai gow is the only game where you can lay your cards on the table and ask the dealer what you should do. The dealer will be more than happy to tell you what they would do with that hand. Remember, the dealer wants you to win. People tip when they win.

4. <u>Don't be the Bank</u>: Pai gow poker offers the opportunity for a player to act as the Bank versus other players and the casino.

In addition to just playing against the dealer, you'll also be playing against all of the other players at the table. Don't do it unless you like taking on everyone else with little chance of winning.

5. <u>Avoid the Dragon:</u> The dragon is a second hand that a player is allowed to play when the game is not full. Don't play the dragon hand, because it requires you to make an entire other bet. If you want to bet more, just make a larger initial bet on one hand.

🍸 Classic Vegas Mistake

Playing at Tables You Can't Afford: Henry walks up to the only table that is open. It's a $25 minimum table, and all the money he has is $100. He does not expect to lose, so he doesn't think he needs a big bankroll. At $25 a hand, all Henry can withstand is a four-card loss swing before he is busted. Five minutes later, he's tapped out. Professionals recommend playing with a bankroll that's ten times the table minimum. Henry should have held out and found a table that met his budget, or just found something else to do.

Sports Wagering

Las Vegas is the only place in the country where you can legally bet on sports. Sports waging is a great way to spend an afternoon with the boys. There are few things better than sitting in a comfy lounge chair, drinking beers, talking sports, and having five important games playing on five different televisions. It's like the ultimate bachelor's living room.

Sports wagers also allow players to get the most out of a single bet, since each bet takes about three hours to complete, and you can enjoy every play of the game because your money is riding on it. So lay your money down and have some fun.

Tips on Playing

1. <u>Stick with the Basics</u>: Don't worry about the five-team parlay, futures, money lines, or even the over/under. Stick with basics – bet the point spreads. A point spread bet is not a bet on whether a team will win, but rather that a team will cover the point differential. For example, a "Broncos minus seven" bet would only win if the Broncos won by more than seven points. If the Broncos won by six points, then the bet would lose. Conversely, on a "Steelers plus seven" bet, the Steelers don't have to win, they just can't lose by more than seven points.

2. <u>Bet in $11 increments</u>: If you win, you get your $11 back plus $10. Any increment other than $11 and you will end up with change and look like you don't know what you are doing.

3. <u>Create Drama</u>: Spread your money over four or five games so you have a bunch of action and drama going on at once. It is fun to have money riding and trying to keep up with multiple games simultaneously.

4. <u>Only Bet on Televised Games</u>: Yes, even though there may be 150 televisions in a sportsbook, there are plenty of games that aren't televised. If you bet on these games you'll miss being able to see your gambling dollars at work. You shouldn't be betting on Grambling versus Slippery Rock anyway; if it's not worth being televised, is it really worth your money?

5. <u>Bet Against New York</u>: If you're looking to place a bet, there are usually good odds against New York teams. There are so many Yankees fans that are going to bet, no matter what the odds are, that the odds against the Yankees are usually pretty good because the sportsbook is looking to cover their bets and not lose their shirts if the New York team wins.

6. <u>Ask for Drink Vouchers</u>: When you are placing a bet, be sure to ask for drink vouchers from the agent. Casinos are clamping down on giving out comp drinks to non-players, so if you order a drink in the sportsbook and don't have a drink voucher, the cocktail server will charge you.

7. <u>Get on the Cocktail Waitress's Good Side:</u> This is very important at a sportsbook. If you get on the cocktail server's good side, she will give you extra drink vouchers. Do this by tipping the amount that the drink would have cost when you use your first voucher. If drinks are normally $4 and you have a voucher, then tip her $4. Your generosity will usually be reciprocated by her giving you additional vouchers as the hours go by.

8. <u>Get a Good Seat</u>: A good seat in a sportsbook is usually hard to find, expect that 75 percent of them will have a "Reserved for Race Players" sign, which means they are off-limits to you. Look for seats that have a view that won't be blocked by pedestrian traffic. If you can't find a seat in the sportsbook, there are usually some good views at the adjacent bar.

Slots and Video Poker

Slots and video poker have taken over casinos; there are miles and miles of slots and video poker. Every day, more table games are taken out and replaced with slots and video poker, which are 24-hour moneymakers. They just plug them in and watch the profits add up. They're popular because a lot of people are intimidated by the table games and don't want to look stupid by committing a breach of gaming etiquette in front of a large crowd. Take your time and learn how to play the real games. Save the video games for when you get home and want to waste time at work.

Who are the Oddsmakers?

You've probably heard the term "Vegas oddsmakers" many times before. Have you ever wondered who the oddsmakers are, and how they arrive at their lines? All opening lines start at the Stardust, which is the sports wagering center of the universe. The guys who run the Stardust sportsbook are considered the primary Vegas oddsmakers. Once the point spreads are set at the Stardust, all the other oddsmakers at other sportsbooks use those lines to start off their point spreads. The oddsmakers are not trying to predict by how much a team is going to win. Rather, they are trying to come up with a point spread that half the bettors will bet for one team while the other half bet on the other team. For example, just because the Colts are favored by five does not mean that the oddsmakers think the Colts will win by five: They set the number five because that is the number it will take for the money to be spread evenly on both sides. If more money were going against the Colts than for the Colts, the oddsmakers would lower the line to four, in hopes of enticing more people to bet on the Colts.

Tips on Playing

1. <u>Avoid</u>: The *Little Black Book* has just one tip on playing slots and video poker: Don't. These games are for old women and social misfits who don't like the friends they came with. Be a man and play table games with the grownups.

Roulette

Roulette is a classic game with a spinning ball and a bunch of numbered, colored squares. If you're looking for something that requires no skill, you've found it. It's an easy game to bet, and an easy game to lose. Here are a couple of tips to keep it pretty exciting.

Tips on Playing

1. <u>The Arrival Bet</u>: Walk into the casino, take all your gambling money, and make one bet on black or red. If you win, blow all your winnings on strippers and drinks, and gamble like you normally would for the rest of your trip. If you lose, don't gamble the rest of the trip. How's that for high stakes?

2. <u>The Departure Bet:</u> There is nothing better than laying down one last bet on roulette when you are leaving town — and winning it. You will walk out of the casino feeling like a king and you'll have a good story to tell when someone asks you "Did you win?" Of course, if you lose you'll board your flight looking just like all of the other miserable losers you'll be traveling home with.

Poker

Are you a guy who wants to hit Vegas to play poker? Read on.

Vegas Poker Rooms

Binion's Horseshoe is home to the World Series of Poker. You probably knew that already. The popularity of this event, plus shows like *The World Poker Tour* and *Celebrity Poker Showdown*, has created a poker renaissance. Perhaps you've watched these shows and thought you could join in on the fun? Before you

♈ Classic Vegas Mistake

Money Handling: Rick walks up to a table, whips out a $100 bill, and hands it to the dealer to get some chips. The dealer looks at him with a blank stare. Rick thinks to himself, why doesn't he take my money? How long to I have to stand here? The rest of the table chuckles, knowing that Rick thinks he is cool but in fact is just embarrassing himself. Rick has made a rookie mistake (hey, we've all been there) and it is this: Dealers in Vegas cannot take money out the hands of patrons. Instead, the money must be placed on the table so the surveillance camera can record the transfer of funds. Don't make this mistake. Put your money on the table like everyone else.

decide to pull up a seat at the table you need to know that there are two different types of poker rooms, the traditional Vegas room and the new Vegas room.

The Traditional Vegas Poker Room

Until recently, the poker room was nothing more to the casino than a pain in the ass. Unlike other table games, where you are playing against the house, in poker you play against other players. The result is, the casino only makes a little off each pot, so they view poker players as an inconvenience. Slot players are treated with much more respect by the casinos, because they put money into their coffers, and poker players don't. Since the poker rooms aren't a significant source of revenue, the casinos don't invest much in them, if they even have one at all.

Playing in the Traditional Poker Room

Traditional poker room action is pathetic. This isn't the World Series, or anything like it. Unless there is a tournament going on, expect it to be very, very quiet and the players to be very old. These rooms are like smoke-filled libraries at a rest home. No one here is drinking booze or out to have a good time. The only beverage being consumed is coffee, and the players here are either: a) professionals who will take your money, or b) retirees who will take your money. Either way you are going to pay for your education in the poker room. You will get a healthy dose of secondhand smoke, but you will not be taking home any pots. If you still aren't convinced that you are going to lose, realize one important thing: Everyone you are playing against comes here every day. The other players will team up just to clean you out. Like your home game, you are playing against other players; unlike your home game, they are all on the same team.

Watching Poker in a Traditional Room

Yes, the poker room is worth looking at, just so you can say you saw it. You can even observe a few hands; notice that your presence agitates the otherwise lifeless players. Perhaps it's a fun story to tell about "the time I played poker at Binion's," but understand that that story will cost you. The *Little Black Book*'s opinion is that the poker room is neither a fun nor memorable experience.

Finding a Traditional Poker Room

The "best" examples of traditional Poker Rooms can be found downtown at Binion's and Fitzgerald's.

New Poker Rooms

On the other end of the poker spectrum are the new rooms. The new rooms are a result of America's poker renaissance. They're sprouting up all over. These rooms are in a fairly prominent part of the casino, not tucked away in a back corner. They're well lit and there's actually some energy in the air.

Playing in the New Poker Rooms

Playing in the new poker rooms isn't easy because they're often very crowded. Everyone wants to play and be seen playing poker. You'll need to put your name on a waiting list, but if you've wanted desperately to prove you're Matt Damon, it's worth the wait. Once you get a seat at the table you'll find the atmosphere is relaxed but upbeat. The new rooms are populated with people like you, not grizzled vets looking to clean you out. Most of the people at these tables are just in town for the weekend and looking to play a few hands, meaning you actually stand a chance of not being played.

Finding a New Poker Room

If you're looking for some action in a new poker room try Bellagio or MGM Grand. Both of these places are good, but crowded.

Tournaments

If you just *have* to play poker, then mini tournaments are the best choice. All the players start at the same time with the same amount of chips. A player is eliminated only when they are out of chips. The game keeps going until there is only one player left at the table. That player is the winner and takes the first-place prize amount.

Other Games

Casinos offer a variety of other games to tempt the players. Groups of guys should not be playing these games; they don't offer the type of experience that you are looking for.

Tips on Other Games

1. <u>Keno</u>: Only play this game if you are sitting bored in a coffee shop and the keno runners are hot. Avoid in all other situations. This is the worst percentage game to play, and you won't have fun sitting in a keno parlor watching numbers appear on a screen.

2. <u>Bingo</u>: If you are down to your last $10 and have an hour to kill, then bingo is the only way to keep gambling. While you won't be enjoying yourself in a completely quiet, smoke-filled room with a bunch of retirees, at least you'll keep on gambling. Well, sort of.

♈ Classic Vegas Mistake

Not Knowing When to Walk Away: It's a lot of fun to watch your friends gamble for a little while, but it's not much fun to watch them for long while. A more pathetic experience is watching people whom you *don't know* gamble. If you've gotten to the point where you're mindlessly observing a businessman from Syracuse play $25 hands of blackjack, it's time to leave the casino. If your bankroll is getting light, move over to the bar and out of the casino. This is easier said than done, since, obviously, if everyone knew when to walk away, the casinos would be out of business, but not walking away when you're not even playing should be a no-brainer. Hang out in the casino only when you're gambling. There are plenty of fun things to do out there, and watching a bunch of strangers at a roulette table isn't one of them. Recently, when we asked friends about their big Saturday night out in Vegas, they said, "I lost big early, so I stood around and watched for a few hours." What a waste of time.

3. <u>Carnival Games</u>: New games offering new ways to gamble your money appear all the time on the gaming floor. The most popular games are Caribbean Stud, Let it Ride, and three card poker. These games are difficult to learn quickly and don't offer a great gambling experience. The rule is: If you don't know how to play it, avoid it.

 WHEN TO PLAY:

Daytime Gambling

Daytime is the best time to gamble on a guys' vacation. Why? Because during the evening the casinos get so crowded that you will not be able to gamble with your friends. During the day, you have a chance to sit at the same table with your friends to play blackjack, craps, or pai-gow.

At night, the table minimums go up. Some of your friends might not be too happy playing blackjack at a minimum of $25 a hand. At those prices, you can guarantee that a few of the guys can't afford to lose for very long without getting upset. And who can blame them? Why throw your money away in large chunks at night when you can have a great time managing your bankroll during the day.

During the day, you and your friends will run an entire table, be able to talk with one another without pissing off everyone else around you, hold epic battles versus the dealer, and pound Heinekens on the casino's tab. So, find a table with a lonely dealer who's just sitting there, and take it over. The same table at night will have a line three deep for every seat.

Tips on Daytime Gambling

1. <u>Find a $5 Blackjack Table.</u> There's no reason to sit at a $10; all you will do is double your losses. If there are no $5 tables fully open and a bunch of open $10 tables all around, tell any pit boss (nicely) that all of you would like to play together at a $5 table. There is a good chance that he will change a $10 table to $5 table, just to get your group to play. If he doesn't, don't feel embarrassed, just thank him and pony up to the casino bar until a $5 table becomes fully open for your crew.

2. <u>Go Manual</u>. If you have a choice between a manual shuffle and an automatic shuffler, go with manual. A manual shuffle is when the dealer has to shuffle by hand. Automatic shufflers do one of two things: continuously shuffle the cards, or prepare new decks of cards while the dealer is dealing the current cards. Yes, it's true that card counters can only work with the manual shuffle, but you should look for a manual shuffle for

your own reasons. A manual shuffle is better than an automatic shuffle because it:

❧ Gives you a natural break to run to the bathroom or tell a story to your friends.

❧ Extends your playtime, allowing you to drink more on the casino's tab, because you aren't playing (and losing) in the extra five minutes it takes for the dealer to shuffle.

3. <u>Get to Know the Dealer</u>. When the dealer is shuffling, break out a conversation and ask a couple of questions. Dealers can help you out by keeping you from making stupid decisions, which will become especially helpful after you have had a couple of drinks.

4. <u>Drink Premium Bottled Beers</u>. You are getting drinks for free, so maximize your value. Instead of ordering a Budweiser or Miller Light, order a Heineken, Sam Adams, or Beck's. Don't order mixed drinks, since casinos are notorious for serving cheap well liquors that will leave you with a nasty hangover. Even though you may ask for Grey Goose, you are going to end up with Popov.

Nighttime Gambling

At night, the tables fill up quickly and table minimums go up. Although it's probably a good idea to restrict your play to earlier in the day, there is definitely a buzz of energy in the casino at night. If you're going to play at night, here are a few things to remember.

Tips on Nighttime Gambling

1. <u>Don't Play in Groups</u>: If you have a group that is trying to gamble at night, you will spend the majority of time walking around trying to find the mythical empty table. Face it, the

place is packed, so if you want to play you'll probably have to fly solo, or at best in groups of two or three.

2. <u>Bring a Larger Bankroll</u>: Table minimums will be up, so bring a larger bankroll with you, otherwise you won't be able to withstand the swings. The swings can be steep, so be prepared to suck it up and lay your money down, otherwise you'll get yourself into a hole without the resources to play your way out.

3. <u>Play in the Party Pit</u>: Some casinos such as Harrah's, Imperial Palace, Stardust, and Rio offer a table games area that also serves as a form of entertainment. Their pit area is swinging, so withdraw your cash, head down, and have a good time.

Late-Night Gambling

In the wee hours of the night/morning, the table minimums go back down and the casinos empty. The late night crowd is usually a wacky bunch. The real boozers have passed out hours ago; this crowd is filled with the socially inept and downright strange. Though we recommend that you should hit the sack or get some food, there are some things you need to look out for when you gamble late at night.

Tips on Late Night Gambling

1. <u>Don't Play Drunk</u>: There is no way to lose your money faster than gambling when you are drunk and tired. At this point you've probably been up for too long and drunk too much to have any chance of playing smart.

2. <u>Don't Play by Yourself:</u> If you look around and notice that you're playing alone at 5 a.m., go to sleep. The dealers don't even look like they want to be there, why should you. If you insist on sticking it out, find a table with at least a few other

players so you can have some sort of interaction. Just be prepared to have some wacko chewing your ear off about his Kennedy assassination theory or how aliens once abducted him.

 WHERE TO PLAY

While the games are the same from casino to casino, the action isn't. There are many places that cater to high rollers and seasoned players. These are the places you probably want to avoid. We're not questioning your gaming "skills," we just want you to go to a place where you and the boys can have a good time.

The key to picking the right place to play is atmosphere. You need to be somewhere upbeat and fun. Generally speaking, seasoned players tend to be pretty mellow at the tables. Fortunes are won and lost and you wouldn't even know it. You need to pick a place where the crowd is raucous and the drinks are plentiful.

Sure Things: Table Games on The Strip

If you decide to stay on the Strip during the day, you have a few great gambling options. The following locations will keep your spirits up and your wallets full. Okay, they won't exactly keep your wallets full, but they will inflict minimal damage.

The Casino Royale

Located between Harrah's and the Venetian, on the Strip, the Casino Royale is a great place for some low-wagering good times in a prime location. Low table minimums at this little gem make for a lively atmosphere. This is the perfect place to spend some hours on games you may be new to, or to try that strategy you've been reading up on. You'll notice that everyone here is having a good time because they aren't losing a lot of money.

There are two table game pits here. Avoid the small pit near the entrance to Outback Steak house — the fun pit is the one that runs along the length of the bar. This pit has a series of low-limit craps, blackjack, roulette, and pai gow poker games. Along the roof are beveled mirrors that allow you to view all of the table action without looking over somebody's shoulder.

Why wait for a waitress to come by for a free drink; they have cheap drinks up at the bar. The standing specials here are $1 Michelob, frozen Rum Runners, and Pina Coladas. You'll see the line of people at the end of the bar waiting for a drink, but don't worry, it moves fast. Grab a drink and hit the tables.

With low drink prices and low table minimums, you get to play, drink, and have fun at a reasonable price. If you are getting free drinks but have to play for $25 a hand to get them, they aren't free.

New Frontier

This casino, mostly known for being home to Gilley's (which features bikini bull riding), offers a good place to play during the day. If you want to catch some of the downtown vibe but don't want to catch a cab, the New Frontier might be the place for you. The $1 frozen margaritas here are larger than the ones you'll find most places on the Strip. The table games usually aren't crowded during the day, providing you and the guys plenty of room to set up shop. It's clean but dated at the Frontier, and there's really nothing wrong with that.

Barbary Coast

If you're of the opinion that the New Vegas is too much like Disneyland, then the Barbary Coast is for you. What puts the Barbary Coast one notch above other throwbacks like the New Frontier and downtown? Location, location, location. This old-school casino has done everything possible to preserve its "vintage" appeal. In other words, they haven't added any of the bells and whistles that make the theme properties so appealing. But hey, if it's cheap drinks, cheap tables, and cheap women you're after, this is the place for you.

Sure Things: Sports Wagering

If you're not a West Coaster, don't forget the time difference. Games start early in Vegas — the NFL starts at 10 a.m., for example. Here are a few sportsbooks that are worth a look-see for groups of guys.

Stardust

One of the only redeeming qualities of the Stardust is its sportsbook. This was one of the first sportsbooks ever, and these days it shows. You won't be watching the games on plasma screens, but you will enjoy the classic sportsbook experience here. The Stardust is the epicenter of sports wagering for the entire country. All of the other casinos — and probably your local bookie — take their cues from this aging casino. When you see the lines, or you hear the term "Vegas oddsmakers," people are talking about the action that starts at the Stardust. Because of its significance to the world of sports wagering, this is *the* haven for hardcore sports gamblers. The regulars at the Stardust know more about sports than the anchors on *Sportscenter* and they're happy to have you join them. They talk it up, share opinions and picks, and keep the energy alive. Before you go, prepare yourself for some in-depth analysis of Peyton Manning playing against a cover-two defense from these Jimmy "the Greek" types.

The Hard Rock

The sportsbook at Hard Rock is small, nice, and low-key. It's worth hanging here if you're staying at the hotel. If you're staying on the Strip but you just want to check the hotel out, watching a game might be just the reason to head over. Plasma screens, excellent cocktail servers, big comfy chairs, and no crowds are what Hard Rock has to offer. Right next to the sportsbook is a sports bar that has six plasmas on the wall, and booth tables with small, personalized televisions. Remember, like Rio and the Palms, Hard Rock is off the Strip and it will take a cab ride to get here. Or, you could walk to Hard Rock to sweat out your hangover.

Mandalay Bay

Mandalay Bay boasts a mammoth sportsbook. On most days, this sportsbook is one of the best because it has lots of televisions, plenty of sitting room and, most importantly, hot, friendly cocktail servers. However, do not make the mistake of heading over here on a huge sports weekend. During March Madness, NFL Play-offs and especially the Super Bowl, this book is a wreck. On big weekends you'll see people lying on the floor because there's no empty seats, the cocktail service is overloaded, there are twenty-minute waits to make bets, and you can't even hear the game because of the deafening roar of the crowd.

MGM Grand

Newly rebuilt in the rotunda area of the casino that meets the Strip, the MGM sportsbook is top of the line in technology. This is a great place to come watch football games on Sunday or basketball during March Madness because there are tons of large plasma TVs offering unobstructed views of the games. The room is set up in three sections of comfortable chairs, each of which has its own cocktail service. It has comfortable booths on the back wall, but people usually walk right in front of you and block your view. A bar and a snack shop are adjacent, making it very easy to get a drink and a bite at halftime.

ESPNZone at New York–New York
Although technically not a sportsbook, this is a great place to have a meal and watch a game. There aren't any cheap drink and eat specials here, but it is a nice environment to check out some action. It gets crowded here, so if you don't have a big party, the staff might seat some strangers next to you to share your booth.

When you secure a booth, take your time ordering. Order one appetizer at a time and for everyone to share. ESPNZone is picky about allowing customers to occupy a booth once they stop drinking or eating. So, take your time, drink the cold beer from their big frosty mugs, munch on some appetizers, and watch the game in a fun, loud, yelling and screaming atmosphere.

The *Little Black Book* knows what you're thinking: If ESPNZone isn't a sportsbook, why are you covering it? Good question. Well, one of the benefits of ESPNZone is that it's probably the only sports viewing locale that actually has women in it. This is where the lady sports fans go to party, and you'll see them in their team jerseys cheering their teams on. If you're a single sports nut, this might be the place for you to pick up. It's pretty easy to approach women when you're both focused on the gaming action. Throw out a soft jab about their team: That should get their attention.

Do Your Homework:
If you're coming to town with the intention of putting some real money into play, make sure you know what you're doing.

Five Gambling Books to Read Before Your Trip:

1. *The Complete Idiot's Guide to Gambling Like a Pro* (Stanford Wong & Susan Spector):

2. *How to Win at Gambling* (Avery Cardoza)

3. *The Unofficial Guide to Casino Gambling* (Basil Nestor)

4. *Guerrilla Gambling* (Frank Scoblete)

5. *The Winner's Guide to Casino Gambling* (Edwin Silberstang)

Gambling Web sites to Visit Before Your Trip:

1. www.thewizardofodds.com

2. www.gamblingtip.net

✴ Chapter 7 ✴

Daytime:
There's More Than Sun to
Soak In During the Day

✴···

While most guys spend their days stuck in a cubicle dreaming of the neon lights of Vegas, they rarely pause to consider how to occupy the hours when the sun is out. Usually the only daytime activities that come to mind involve the pool, or golf. The *Little Black Book* covered the pool in "Accommodations." Since hotel pools are strictly for guests only, and Las Vegas has no municipal pools near the Strip, if you didn't consider the pool when you booked your reservations, you might as well forget it now.

However, since Vegas is a 24-hour town, pretty much anything you'd want to do late at night you can do during the day, too, and usually with smaller crowds and lower minimums. So don't sleep all day: Get the guys up, out of their rooms, and head out onto the street. Some of your best options for gaming, drinking, and carousing await you while the sun is high.

> ### 🍸 Classic Vegas Mistake
>
> **Vegas Golf:** Most guys love golf, and what's not to love? You get to spend time flexing your expensive new driver and trying out some jokes you just ripped off from Jon Stewart. You and the guys can throw back a few beers and have a really good time. Sure, what's not to love about golf? In Vegas, everything.

10 Reasons to Avoid Playing Golf in Vegas

1. Las Vegas is in the desert.

Don't be fooled by the fountains at Bellagio: You're in a parched wasteland. It's hotter than hell trying to play golf in this town.

2. Las Vegas *is in the desert.*

Just wanted to make sure you got the point. If you didn't, here are some others to dissuade you.

3. Someone's going to bail.

One of your friends had too much to drink last night and stayed out way too late. What does this mean to you? At least one no-show. That's right; while he's sleeping it off, your foursome is going to get paired up with some random loser who couldn't find three friends to play a round of golf with.

4. Good Las Vegas Golf Is Not Next to the Strip.

The best Vegas golf courses are at least a twenty-minute cab ride away. You'll pay a small fortune in cab fare just getting to and from the course.

5. Golf in Las Vegas Is Expensive.

How expensive? Be prepared to shell out at least five times what you pay at your local municipal course. The courses here know that if you are willing to travel off the Strip to play a round, they can charge whatever they want. You, my out-of-state friend, are their lifeblood.

6. The Good Tee Times Are Hard to Get.

If you don't heed the *Little Black Book*'s advice and avoid golf altogether, make your reservations early. Most of the good early tee times, the ones where you can finish before it gets to be over 110 degrees, are booked way in advance. The best tee times are reserved for casino high-rollers and locals. You will most likely get stuck with a tee time that will make you think you're on the surface of the sun by the time you tee off at number three.

7. It won't take up half your day, it will take up your *whole* day.
Between the distance and the amount of time it takes to play a round of golf, you will be spending your entire day doing this. And face it, you're going to return to your hotel sunburned, tired, and dehydrated.

8. Can't you play golf at home?
Are you really willing to spend a lot of time, money, and energy on something that you could do next Saturday? Besides, if you wait until you get home to play a round, you'll have plenty of good Vegas stories to tell your friends.

9. Bringing golf clubs on a plane is a pain in the ass.
If you decide to bring your clubs, you'll have to check your bags, which will add forty-five minutes of waiting in the airport after you plane arrives. Plus, when you depart Las Vegas, be prepared to get to the airport two hours in advance, just so your bags make it on the plane. Lose the clubs; carry-on is the only way to go. Your time is precious in Vegas; don't waste it caddying your clubs around.

10. Vegas golf is overrated.
Like many things in Vegas, the golf courses don't live up to their billing. What you will hear about is amazing courses with unbelievable views, but what you will normally find are packed courses, with houses lining every fairway and bunker. Real estate on golf courses is hot in Vegas, but the courses themselves rarely are. Sure, there are some amazing places to play, but playing them means reserving early, wasting a day, and shelling out some serious cash.

So, you decided to pass on golf. Good. With so much else to do in Las Vegas during the day, you've made the right decision. Now let's have some real fun.

🚌 DOWNTOWN BY DAY

Most guys have visions of downtown Las Vegas that include hard drinking, hard living, and hard women. If that's what you're looking for downtown, you're destined to find it. Downtown doesn't mess around.

The appeal of downtown is that it doesn't hide behind a squeaky clean facade. Downtown is just plain, good old-fashioned gambling, with unhealthy doses of smoking, drinking, and trashy women thrown in for good measure.

The downtown casinos are the product of a different era. Most of them were built during the 1950s, when Vegas was just a place for adult vice. The buildings here were designed for gambling; hotels and restaurants were nothing more than a necessary evil. The downtown casinos, which are an assembly of joints that line Fremont Street, lack any element of pageantry or showmanship. These places seem dingy compared to the well-polished action on the Strip; you won't find animatronic shows here. However, what downtown lacks in elegance, it more than makes up for in character.

Downtown will remind East Coasters of Atlantic City. The gambling halls on Fremont Street are right next to one another; you don't have to walk a half mile to go from one property to the next. All of the casinos are products of pre-Strip design. They have low ceilings — something you'll notice the second you walk in. The low ceilings make the gaming floor feel cramped, and they trap smoke so there is a thick haze as far as the eye can see, which isn't too far. Because the buildings aren't too large, they don't employ the open floor plan of the Strip properties: Every square inch of space is used downtown, and the games are packed in real tight. There aren't as many gimmicky games here; these casinos focus on the gaming classics: blackjack, roulette, and craps.

Spend a few hours downtown. It won't cost you a ton of money, you'll be able to gamble with friends and you'll see old-school Vegas.

Getting There

The best way to get downtown is by cab. It's not cheap to get there, but if you're staying for more than two days, or have a burning desire to see old-school Vegas, this trip is a must. This is one of the few things that might make you wish you'd rented a car.

Parking Downtown

If you do have a car, park at the valet at the Horseshoe. It'll only set you back the cost of a tip. If you don't valet, you'll have to park in their mammoth parking garage, which puts you a long walk away from the casino, and you'll have to get your ticket validated at one of the few nondescript validation machines inside the casino, or otherwise it will cost you $5.

Sure Things Downtown:

Before you arrive, scan through the "Sure Things" and hash out a plan of action. There is no single must-see attraction; it's the little things that make downtown special.

Binion's Horseshoe

Start your trek here. The action is at the front of the casino by the craps tables. Since $2 minimums are common here, start with a $20 bill and let the dice fall as they may. Playing craps at Binion's will give you a real taste of old-school Vegas. The dealers at Binion's are friendly and seem to have a real passion for what they do. Also, if you're looking for single or double deck blackjack, this is a great place to play.

There are two bars here at the Horseshoe. Avoid the one lining the back of the casino; this is where you should go and drink away your sorrows if you just lost your child's college fund. It is a truly miserable experience. But hey, if you are into that, this is your place. Otherwise, hit the small bar by the sportsbook; it is great for a stiff drink. Don't sit, stand behind the stools so you can turn around to the open-air entrance and watch the passersby. They usually have a $1 beer special, so ask the bartender before you order. Since you are at the Horseshoe, Jack Daniels, straight up, is the recommended spirit. Down a shot and watch the hair grow on your chest.

If you're hungry, whatever you do, stay away from the deli in the back. It's possibly the worst that the *Little Black Book* has ever seen.

The Golden Nugget

The Nugget, aside from being the location of Fox's forgettable show *The Casino,* is notable for being the first property managed by Vegas pioneer Steve Wynn. Known for his exacting standards, Wynn made the Nugget into a first-class property. The Nugget is old, but it's nice. There isn't too much to see here, but since you're already downtown, you might as well stop in. Put a dollar in the "Big Bertha" slot machine next to the door and watch in amazement as huge reels spin and land on nothing. Don't expect to win on this machine; it has the worst payments in the building.

Mermaids

Mermaids is one of the many Vegas attractions that advertises giant margaritas. Although we're not sure just how much alcohol is in them, it's our guess there's probably not enough to wash out a paper cut.

Aside from the giant margaritas, Mermaids is home to that culinary sensation sweeping the nation: the deep-fried, chocolate-covered Twinkie. There's nothing good that can be said about these harbingers of heart disease, but that doesn't mean they can't be fun. Since it's Vegas, and everyone is in a betting mood, why not bet one another who can down the most of these bad boys. We think it's safe to say this is a bet where everyone loses.

Mermaids also sells cheap Mardi Gras beads. The ladies (a term that can only be used loosely to describe downtown's female denizens) love 'em. Buy some and see what type of action you can scare up. The *Little Black Book* has had success getting the full Mardi Gras reaction. That's right: women seem to be willing to flash for beads just about everywhere — *Girls Gone Wild* Fremont Street-style. If you attract attention from more than the ladies, namely casino security or Johnny Law, we never gave you this suggestion in the first place. Remember: downtown is the bail bonds center of Las Vegas, so you probably won't be locked up too long, and boy will you have a story for your next poker night.

The Four Queens
Another great example of old-school Vegas, the Four Queens is a downtown legend. The ceilings are a little higher here, so you might be able to get a few breaths in before you succumb to the secondhand smoke. This is a fun place to gamble because it's home to a lot of low stakes play, which usually keeps both the employees and the customers in a good mood.

As you head deeper into the casino it becomes jam-packed with old slot machines and even older ladies with oxygen tanks, so stay near the entrances to Fremont Street. If you're up for a drink, stop by the bar at the Chicago Brewing Company.

Main Street Station
A little bit off of Fremont Street, this is probably the best mix of cleanliness and fun downtown. The best part of Main Street Station is the Triple Seven Brewpub. It delivers a solid microbrew and offers a perfect atmosphere to watch a sporting event.

You Gotta See This: Out in the casino, the men's room features a huge chunk of the Berlin Wall that you can relieve yourself on. You can't do that back in Poughkeepsie, so load up on the beer and take your best shot.

 DAYTIME DIVERSIONS:

If you've done enough gambling for the day, if gambling isn't your thing, or if you just want to take a break, here are a few great adventures to make your trip memorable.

Daiquiri Dash:

If you are thirsty or sober you are ready to begin the Daiquiri Dash. It is really more of a Daiquiri Drunken Walk/Stumble than a Dash. The Dash is a walking trip up the east side of the Strip drinking frozen drinks, stopping for refills at cheesy drink places the whole way up. It's a great way to beat the heat, see the Strip and meet some ladies. The frozen beverages will keep you cool in the desert sun, and there's plenty of time for scotch on the rocks tonight.

Begin: Fat Tuesday's at MGM

Fat Tuesday's is located in the bowels of the MGM Grand. Take the escalator just off the main lobby down to the parking garage and look for Tuesday's at the bottom of the escalator. Buy a 16-ounce "190 Octane" and a few Jell-O shots for the ladies. Once you've made some new friends and are ready to hit the road, hug the left-hand side of the lobby and proceed into the casino. After you pass Tabu, MGM's ultralounge, take a hard left and keep walking. In about two minutes, on your left, you'll see the lion habitat, a large glass enclosure featuring two (sleeping) lions. Take a quick peak at the lions as you enter the large, circular room. Don't go up the escalators; instead, stay on the main floor and cross the circular room to

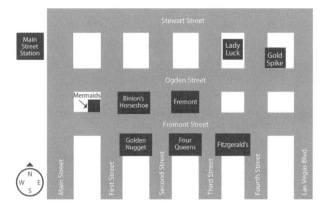

The Ladies of Fremont

Fremont attracts a lower class of woman than the Strip. That may sound horribly politically incorrect, but take a look around. You won't find Miss Pampered L.A. here; instead, you'll find the kind of gal who can open a beer bottle with her teeth. Although they are a little rough, the ladies of Fremont Street are a lot of fun. These are the girls that you'll blow off until 4 a.m., when you get back from a strip club and are ready to make a frantic last-ditch phone call. Perhaps you should spend some time now getting a few phone numbers for later in the evening. Buckle up and enjoy the ride.

a Strip exit. Once you're outside, take a right on the sidewalk and stumble forward. Get past MGM and get ready for a refill at your next stop.

Stop 1: La Salsa Cantina

La Salsa Cantina is a cheesy Mexican restaurant/bar on the Strip. This isn't a place to hang out, but it serves as a good refill station. This is the one place where The *Little Black Book* recommends buying a yard of margarita, because here you actually get your money's worth. The next leg of your journey will take you through a dead part of the Strip where you won't see anyone that will make you feel embarrassed about drinking from a cheesy, three-foot-tall mug. Once you leave La Salsa Cantina, walk past GameWorks, the M&M Factory, the Coca-Cola bottle, Fatburger, dingy souvenir shops, and mini-marts.

Stop 2: Hawaiian Market Place

As you pass the last minimart, you'll see the Hawaiian Marketplace on your right. The Hawaiian Marketplace is a covered outdoor "village" sandwiched between the Polo Towers and the Harley-Davidson Café. Before you get a drink, walk into the village's center circle. The circle is the place to be every hour, as a troupe of Hawaiian dancers perform a show. About fifteen minutes into the show, the Hawaiian dancers pull members of the audience in to teach them how to dance. The male dancers always pull in a couple of attractive twenty to thirty year-old women. If they pick some cute female volunteers who catch your eye, don't hesitate, join in the fun. Nothing helps you bond with attractive strangers quite like engaging in a silly dance together. It only lasts about three minutes or so, but that three minutes is all you need. Once it ends, walk off with the women and have a good laugh about how much fun it was.

A frozen libation is a great way to extend the good time. Offer to buy the ladies a drink at the Tiki Hut, located near the front of the marketplace. Don't worry about seeing the end of the show — the rest is all for little kids. Be sure to go into the hut to buy your drinks so you can spend time getting to know your new friends in a more intimate setting. If you buy them outside, the girls will say thanks for the free drinks and keep on moving. The *Little Black Book* says go with a pina colada here because it contains a pineapple wedge that might help to counteract the negative effects of all that booze you've been chugging down. Okay, it probably won't, but at least you're consuming something that's healthy-ish. Now, convince the women to join you guys on the rest of your journey.

Continue up the Strip, passing the Harley-Davidson café, Paris (walk underneath the Eiffel Tower), Bally's and Barbary Coast. This will be your longest walk between pit stops, so be sure to leave the Hawaiian Marketplace with a full drink.

Stop 3: The Daiquiri Bar in front of Margaritaville

At the end of the next casino, the Flamingo, is Jimmy Buffet's Margaritaville Café. Don't bother heading into the main bar: Margaritaville doesn't get hopping until later at night. Instead, head to the Daiquiri Bar just beyond the main entrance. Refill here and head out to the small terrace. It's a nice perch to overlook the ladies passing by on the Strip. After you've hung out for a while, maybe made a couple of catcalls that make you sound like a drunken construction worker, down your drink and press on to the next stop.

Try this: Before you go in, wait for some girls to come get close, smile at them and say "Who wants margaritas?" in a joking way. Remember, most of the girls walking by are usually bored and looking for something to do, so there is a good chance that one of them will say, "I do." If they do, lure the whole group through the doors into the Daiquiri Bar. If they don't, lure yourself into the bar.

Stop 4: The Daiquiri Bar outside Tequila Joe's

Located just outside Tequila Joe's, the Daiquiri Bar is a nice pit stop. Be sure to flash tip money as they're pouring your drink to get a little extra booze in your blend. Once you've filled up, grab a seat at Tequila Joe's. This is a great spot to people-watch. Everyone who enters the Imperial Palace has to pass through Joe's. You'll notice, however, that that is exactly what most people do. Few stop in for a drink, which is unfortunate, because this a fun, low-key stop along the Strip.

Upon leaving Tequila Joe's, head out onto the Strip. You'll pass Harrah's, Casino Royale, and the Venetian toward your destination, TI. At the Venetian, cross over the Strip to TI.

End: Sirens Outdoor Drink Stand at TI

You've made it, this is your destination. Walk past the valet entrance to the TI center entrance (next to the ships). As you approach, you'll see a stand with attractive women doling out the last of your daiquiris. The drinks here aren't the strongest, but at this point you really shouldn't need much more help.

If it's late in the afternoon, you might be just in time for the first show of the night. The show *Sirens of TI* is free, and the first performance is at 7 p.m. In this outdoor adventure, a group of beautiful sirens lure a band of evil pirates from their cove, to a watery grave. Yes, this is a must see in Vegas, but make sure you stay within arm's length of the bar, because standing around in a crowd waiting for the pirates to arrive is really boring.

By the way, did you notice that you've seen some of the interesting sights along the Strip? Between Tabu, the Eiffel Tower, the outdoor canal at the Venetian, and Hula dancers at Hawaiian Village, you've seen a lot of neat places, and maybe later in your trip you can actually bother to go into some of them.

Thrill Seeker Trifecta

Any guy who reckons himself a bit of an adrenaline junky has to say he's done Insanity at Stratosphere, the Manhattan Express

Lead them to the Promised Land

Maybe you aren't much of a ladies' man back home, or perhaps you're a bit shy, but here, it doesn't matter. Often the packs of women roaming up and down the Strip are a bit bored and directionless. If you propose to provide them fun, you might be surprised at just how many takers you'll get.

Vegas is a town built on distraction, and it often becomes overwhelming to newcomers. You see people wandering around like zombies, and it isn't because they've had too much to drink, lost their life savings, or haven't slept in three days. It's because their body went into stimulation overload. All the neon signs, buildings, and walkways have taken their toll on these hapless travelers. They want to have fun, but they don't know where to turn. There are just too many options, so they wander around, victims of option paralysis, unable to commit to anything. Throw them a lifeline: use The *Little Black Book* to provide direction to the directionless. The book's given you a plan, share it with the ladies, and you'll be rewarded.

roller coaster at New York–New York, and SPEED the Ride roller coaster at the Sahara. It makes for a great story, even though you might get a bit queasy. Cut back on the booze before this side trek, or things could get a bit messy.

New York–New York's Manhattan Express:

Begin or end here. The other two are at the very end of the Strip. The Manhattan Express will set you back anywhere from $5 to $20; the price for a ride varies, depending on demand. This roller coaster is extremely popular, so the line can be unwieldy at times. If the zigzagging line occupies more than half the room, come back another time. Although this coaster is fun, it isn't worth waiting an hour for.

Don't be fooled by its age; although this coaster is new, it ain't smooth, plus it reaches speeds of up to 70 miles per hour. The Manhattan Express achieves engineering feats usually found on larger coasters. What does that mean to the riders? This is a fast and hard ride — it's not an ultra-smooth mega coaster, the likes of which you'd find at Six Flags.

While you are standing around in line with a bunch of twelve year-olds, you will probably be thinking, What the hell am I doing here? Don't worry, this is one of Vegas's must-dos — you won't regret it.

The coaster offers a dramatic view of the Strip. As you ascend the first hill, it is a surreal moment as you look out over the turrets of Excalibur. The ride brings you around to the front of New York-New York and swings by the side of MGM Grand. With the Strip below you and hundreds of people staring up, this experience is one for the memory books. This coaster would probably be average if it were located in an amusement park, but it's not; instead, it overlooks the one and only Las Vegas Strip, giving it high marks in the The *Little Black Book*.

The Sahara's SPEED the Ride:
At the Sahara, you can try out this coaster that truly lives up to its name. At one point it accelerates from 35 to 70 miles per hour in two seconds. This is about as intense a thrill ride as you'll find anywhere.

Getting to this ride is kind of a pain; proceed from the front of the hotel to the left corridor. Walk through a series of small slot machine rooms and through the downstairs bar of the NASCAR Café. On your left-hand side is SPEED the Ride, which will set you back $10. But, if you think you have what it takes to do it again, SPEED allows you to go as many times as you want in a row. Few make it more than twice before they puke. You think you are a thrill seeker and have a good stomach? Bet your friends that whoever rides the most wins a lap dance. After two trips, stop; let your friends keep going and battle it out. WARNING: They will be sick, but it will make for a good story.

Stratosphere:
When it comes to Vegas thrill rides, Stratosphere is the best. Their rides are located atop the Stratosphere Tower, over 900 feet above the Strip. Tops on the list is Insanity.

Insanity:
Insanity is an apt name for this ride, which allows ten riders to strap into seats that are suspended by a giant arm that swings out over the Strip. The seats all face one another, forming a circle. Once the arm extends over the side of the building, the seats start whirling as the circle expands and riders spin at speeds up to 40 miles per hour.

Getting There:
Once you enter the Stratosphere there are two ways to the Tower: the short way and the long way. Don't follow the signs; they'll send you up a double escalator and through a winding catacomb of boring retail space. Instead, follow all signs leading to Hamada's, their sushi place. You'll pass the main cage on your left, then an empty lounge bar on your right. Before you get to Hamada's, you will go down a couple of steps that bring you into a new room with a single escalator. This escalator is a shortcut around the mall and will save you a good ten minutes and a lot of walking.

At the top of the escalator you will see the elevators to the Stratosphere Tower. You have to buy a ticket to ride the elevators. Before you buy anything, check the line. If the line is longer than forty people, don't buy a ticket. The long line probably means that the Tower is closed; it shuts down frequently and doesn't reopen for hours. Although the Tower is closed, Stratosphere will keep selling tickets to go up the elevators. Hundreds of people each day buy tickets to the Tower, just to get frustrated by the delays and decide to leave. There are no refunds.

If you were lucky enough to get to the top of the tower, proceed to the rides entrance. It will bring you up an elevator where you will alight atop the observation deck, at the true top of the tower. There is usually a five-minute line here. Five minutes is just long enough for your heart to start racing and a sizable lump in your throat to build up. Once you are strapped in, just realize you are helpless. You won't be able to look straight down, so it feels like you are 1,000 feet up with nothing beneath you. There will be a lot of teenage girls crying after each ride. You can cry, too, if you don't mind the fact that your friends will never, ever let you live it down.

The Real Man's Day Spa

This little daytime diversion will get you ready for a Rat Packer's night on the town by making you feel like a million bucks. All of the locations you'll hit are in Mandalay Bay.

The Art of Shaving: Barber Spa

Book an appointment at The Art of Shaving: Barber Spa in advance, it's very popular. Here you'll be able to get an old-school, straight-blade shave. You probably haven't had one of these before, and if you have, it's probably been a while, so part with the $25 and enjoy. This is no ordinary shave, by any means; when was the last time you spent a half hour shaving? That's right, thirty minutes of pampering you won't soon forget. They start by warming your face with a hot towel, then apply some shaving cream and whip out the straight razor. After they apply their ointments, balms and oils you'll feel like Al Capone in *The Untouchables*. Uh, no . . . wait, that's the one where he gets nicked when he's getting a shave, isn't it? Oh well, you get the point.

Davidoff Cigars:

Pick up a cigar or two for your night on the town. This place is not cheap, but hey, you can smoke the Swisher Sweets at home.

A Journey to the Kitschy Part of the Strip: At least one of the guys in your party will want to check out the kitschy part of the Strip. Just remember there is a thin line between kitschy and pathetic. Westward Ho, Slots-A-Fun, and Circus Circus are just plain pathetic. These three sideshow attractions at the end of the Strip will take the wind out of your sails, really fast. All three seem to be competing for the best hot dog deal on the planet, and although it's unfair to declare a winner, it's probably best to avoid all of them. Westward Ho's showroom/bar usually features one of the worst Elvis impersonators that you'll ever find. The patrons of these places will most likely remind you of everyone you've ever seen on *America's Most Wanted*.

Circus Circus in particular is one to steer clear of during the day. While the steak house here is great at night, avoid the big top when the sun is out. If you're a dad, the last thing you want on your vacation with the boys is to endure the sounds of a bunch of screaming kids. If you don't have kids, five minutes in Circus Circus will make you start saving up for a vasectomy. Oh, yeah: If you do decide to go down to this part of the Strip, see which one of your friends is man enough to try the 99-cent shrimp cocktail, a unique treat that is easy on the wallet and tough on the stomach.

You'll bust one of these babies out when you're swigging down a scotch on the rocks later tonight. Then again, there's no rule that says you can't enjoy one right now.

55 Degrees:
Stop in to this wine store and proceed to the Italian section. Pick out a $20 bottle of Barolo. Bust it out tonight for a nice little pre-dinner toast with the fellas, while you're getting ready for a night on the town. The staff will wrap your bottle in a funky tubing

that will get you noticed in the casino as a man of refined tastes (if that's the look you're going for).

Shoe Shine:
Proceed down the escalator to the casino, then walk past the sportsbook until the carpet ends. To your right is a shoe shine service. The best shoe shine service in town. Why is it the best? Because you are aloft, above everybody, giving you a great chance to do some people-watching. Take a puff on your cigar, kick back, and enjoy yourself. Once you're done getting your shoes shined, you'll look and feel like a million.

Shoot 'Em Up

Interested in something you can't do at home? Unless home is Detroit, chances are you haven't ever had the chance to shoot an assault rifle before. Wanna try one? You'll need to catch a cab, because this adventure takes place three and a half miles off the Strip at The Gun Store.

The Gun Store will allow you a chance to rent several different machine guns. That's right, machine guns. You'll have the opportunity to take target practice with an M16, AK-47, and Uzi 9MM. These are the real deal: something the kick will make you realize the second you pull the trigger. In addition to the rifles, you can fire off a few rounds Dirty Harry-style with .357 and .44 Magnums. If you were looking for another Vegas story to tell the guys back home, I think you found it. Be sure to make a reservation in advance: This is a popular pastime.

One Last Chance

If you failed to bring everything on the *Little Black Book*'s checklist from "Rally Your Troops," and neglected to bring something decent to wear tonight, you still have a chance. Check out the

Forum Shops at Ceasars Palace, the Desert Passage at Aladdin, or Grand Canal Shoppes at the Venetian. There are plenty of places in these malls to buy some decent duds. Remember, you have to dress the part. What's the point of the *Little Black Book* telling you where to go out if you're going to dress like a schmo? You're better than that.

Head on Out

As you head back toward your room to prepare for your night on the town, pick up some fixin's to make a pre-night-out cocktail. Afterward, go back to your room, take a nap, get a shower, get dressed, and get ready to head out for a good time.

✶ Chapter 8 ✶

Nighttime: Things Really Heat Up When the Sun Goes Down

✶··

Once the sun finally creeps down behind Luxor and fades into oblivion, the Strip is ready to turn it up. Since the town seems to go all out every night, having a good time in Vegas isn't hard. But who wants good? You want *great*. There's a lot of things to pack into your nighttime pleasure trip through Sin City; that said, you need to plan ahead. The great times won't find you, you need to go out and get them. Trust us, you'll have great stories to tell, a silly grin plastered over your face, and will be in dire need of sleep once we're through with you.

Plan Ahead

What happens if you fail to plan ahead? Here's a typical sight: a group of guys (who look shockingly like you and your pals!) wandering up and down the Strip looking for "action." Take a look around: This town is loaded with guys, all in the same boat. Everyone is wandering aimlessly, and all the while the clock is ticking. Your caravan heads from one hotel to the next, never completely satisfied with the "action" that you come across, always looking for something better. Eventually the long day catches up with you, and you call it a night. Kind of lame, huh? Don't let this happen to you. Take time at lunch to set up the night's events, make some calls, and do your homework. Get everyone on the same page or you'll all be wandering off in different directions. What follows in this chapter are some of the best evening activities for groups of guys that will kick your trip into overdrive.

 ## NIGHTCLUBS AND BARS

The Vegas bar scene is second to none. Just like everything else, it's on a scale that puts every other city to shame. Sure, there are plenty of bars in New York or Chicago, but they look like shoeboxes compared with the places we'll take you to. The nightclub scene is hot — it's like South Beach out here, with a new place opening every week. However, we're going to go out on a limb and suggest you forego the clubs this trip. Here's why.

Avoid Nightclubs

Nightclubs can be a lot of fun, but are they really fun for a group of guys? A large group of guys has special needs that don't fit well with the agenda at nightclubs. Here are a few things to consider:

- **You're with a bunch of guys**. Kind of obvious, but it's worth pointing out that you don't stand much of a chance getting into a decent club with your pals. Any good club wants a high girl-to-guy ratio, as quoted from one club manager: "We try to maintain a four woman to one man ratio. The one man we let in should be able to afford the four women." They don't want a sausage factory crowding the dance floor, so you don't stand much of a chance. Is it really worth suffering the humiliation of waiting forever, hoping that the bouncers will take pity on you and let you in?

- **Cover charge**. If by some miracle you are given the opportunity to get in with the guys, expect it to cost you big. The bouncers don't mind making an occasional exception for a group of guys, but it has to come at the right price. So buck up and don't be surprised if you have nothing left over to buy a drink once you get it. Besides, even if you get a chance to bribe your way in, you need to ask yourself what's on the other side of that velvet rope? It might put you in mind of the famous Groucho Marx line: "I refuse to join any club that would have someone like me as a member."

♣ **Too loud to talk to anyone.** Any decent club has a sound system that prevents you from carrying on a conversation. Did you really fly all this way to go hang out with friends that you can't even talk to?

♣ **Too crowded.** Do you like bumping into people, fighting your way through a crowd just to find a place to stand? That's the typical club environment. The only area that's not overcrowded is the VIP area, and trust us, you're not getting in there.

♣ **You won't land any girls.** The girls at clubs are not the ones for you. These girls either came with a really rich guy or are there to dance. You won't be able to pick them up at the bar, because they don't even go to the bar. If you want to stand a chance, you have to get right in there and dance, and odds are excellent you *can't* dance. One reason they go to clubs is that it's so loud, they won't be bothered by guys like you trying to make small talk.

♣ **Tough to get a drink.** The bar is packed, and the bartenders won't give you the time of day unless you flash some cash.

♣ **Getting a seat is expensive.** You want to sit down? Be prepared to buy a table. Even if there are any available, tables come with a bottle minimum: usually one bottle for every two people. With bottles at $300, that would be $1,200 for group of eight.

Face it, hitting a club on this trip is a bad idea. Save it for sometime when you've got a hot date you want to impress, but for now, save yourself time, money, frustration, and humiliation: don't bother.

$$$ IF MONEY IS NO OBJECT

The Reserved Table and Bottle Service: Bottle service is taking the Vegas nightclub industry by storm. Clubs have realized they can make more money by selling bottles at huge premiums versus individual drinks at small markups. So, if you really want to hit a club, call the club a day before and buy a table. There usually will be a two- or three-bottle minimum, but your group can go straight to the VIP entrance and not have to worry about fighting your way to the front of the line and tipping the bouncer. If yours is a once-in-a-lifetime trip, perhaps it's worth it. Just remember: It's an experience your credit card will be carrying for months (or years) to come. If you want to go this route, the best places to do so are Light at the Bellagio, Tabu at MGM Grand, MIX at Mandalay Bay, or Vivid at the Venetian.

Hit the Bars Instead: Choosing the Right One for Your Crew

The *Little Black Book* will point you to top places built for groups of guys. A place where you can go, get a drink (okay, several), not wait in line and, most importantly, have a chance of meeting choice women. Since nightclubs are a non-starter, your best option is a bar that has a great party scene. Trust us, they won't remind you of your corner bar at home. Your hometown bar probably has a sixty-five-year-old ex-merchant marine permanently positioned at the end seat who's always going on about "this amazing woman I met in Fiji in 1969," and a mechanic who's an addictive gambler and never seems to have ever picked the right game in his life.

A Vegas bar is a completely different scene. Vegas bars are full of young, good-looking people out to have a great time. There are not a lot of bitter divorcees here, just people in town for some serious fun. (Okay, there are plenty of bitter divorcees in Vegas, but they don't tend to party it up on the Strip.) Here are a few key factors in determining the best place to whoop it up.

The Criteria of a Good Guy's Nighttime Venue

1. <u>Cheap and Easy Entry.</u> You need to be able to get your whole group in the door without any trouble, and a low or — even better — no entry fee is a must.

2. <u>Party Atmosphere.</u> A good Vegas bar is full of people out to have a great time, not people looking to drown their sorrows after they got cleaned out at the blackjack table. You need a place with that party atmosphere.

3. <u>Lots of Good-Looking Women.</u> There needs to be a large number of women who fit the universally accepted general guidelines for attractiveness. You know 'em when you see 'em.

4. <u>Accessible Women.</u> It needs to be a place full of woman who are carefree, approachable and out to meet guys. It's no use having a lot of women on the premises if you don't stand a chance of actually talking to one.

5. <u>Seating.</u> You need a place where your buddies can set up a base camp for the night. The right place is one where you can get a big table where everyone can kick back with a few drinks and soak up the action.

6. <u>Noise Level.</u> It needs to be loud enough to keep the party pumping, but you have to be able to carry on a conversation without yelling at one another.

Bar	Location	Entry	Party	# of Women	Accessible Women	Seating	Noise	TOTALS
Carnival Court	Harrah's	8	10	10	10	8	7	53
Kaunaville	TI	10	7	7	9	10	8	51
Voodoo Lounge	Rio	7	10	8	10	6	9	50
Dueling Piano Bar	NY–NY–	6	10	10	7	7	6	46
House of Blues	Mandalay	7	8	8	7	8	8	46
Margaritaville	Flamingo	9	7	8	6	6	9	45
Dueling Piano Bar	Harrah's	10	9	7	6	7	6	45
The Oasis Lounge	Mandalay	10	5	6	6	9	8	44
The Beach	Off Strip	7	8	7	8	6	7	43
Cleopatra's Barge	Caesar's	9	7	6	6	7	7	42

☑ THE *LITTLE BLACK BOOK*'S LUCKY 7 BARS FOR GROUPS OF GUYS

1. Carnival Court at Harrah's: The Tops

This open-air bar is the embodiment of Vegas fun. It's one of the best times in Vegas, period.

Entry: There is usually a small line to get in. The cover charge for men can range from $2 to $5 — one of the best deals in town.

Party: A full-out party at the bar area, with flare bartenders who juggle their bottles *Cocktail* style, sing, dance, and occasionally breathe fire. Onstage, expect to find cheesy bands and lounge singers. Everyone here is out to have some fun. In addition, if some of your group just has to gamble and does not want to leave the tables, the whole group will like it here because Carnival Court has blackjack tables inside the venue.

Number of Women: Plentiful. Most of them are Midwestern girls who have probably been out drinking all day.

Accessible Women: The dance floor is a great spot to pick up. There are tons of girls dancing all around looking to meet guys. All you need to do is bust out some of your lame moves and they'll be all over you. Trust us, they're not looking for a guy who can dance, because they certainly can't. The second-best place to pick up is the bar. The girls love the bar here because the bartenders reel them in with their theatrics. Stay on the outside of the bar, where you'll be able to get a good look at the ladies. If you make the mistake of sitting directly at the bar, you'll be stuck facing inward with no ability to scope the scene.

Seating: Lots of tables make it easy to set up shop.

Noise: It is almost too loud around the bar, but if you step away from it a bit, you can carry on a conversation.

2. Kaunaville at TI: Post-Show Party Central

This bar directly across from the entrance to Mystere heats up when the show lets out. There's lots of fun to be had, and it's really not a far walk from Carnival Court, so start out there and then head over to Kaunaville.

Entry: No line, and it's free. Just walk in the door and head over to the bar.

Party: The party is tops once the show lets out and people have had a chance to get a couple of drinks in them. During the other times, Kanunaville is a chill place to kick back some cold ones away from the gaming action.

Number of Women: This place has a solid offering, but you'll probably find that each group of woman usually has one or

Nighttime 159 ♣

two guys with them. So, your cheesy Vegas pickup lines probably won't work here.

Accessible Women: The bartenders will help you out here. Have them make some extravagant shots and send them over to the girls; make sure you order an extra for yourself and head on over with shot in-hand.

Seating: Lots of places to find a seat at the bar or at a table. Just don't sit at the back side of the bar, because your entire view will be blocked by big slushy machines.

Noise: It gets loud during the bartenders' show, but other than that it is manageable.

3. Voodoo Lounge at the Rio: Getting Down on the Roof

Located on the roof of the Rio, the Voodoo is a nice mix of lounge party and outside dance floor. Voodoo is the one place that offers the look and feel of a nightclub without being one.

Entry: At $20 a head for men, this is the most expensive of our nighttime recommendations. The line takes a couple of minutes as they check IDs and collect payment. Once you pay, head over to the glass elevator and on up to the roof. Be sure to make some small talk for the benefit of the women in the elevator so if you see them later, it won't be a cold introduction.

Party: On the inside, the lounge band's set list will bring you back to your high school prom. On the outside, a DJ plays hip-hop and dance music. Everywhere you look there are people having a good time.

Number of Women: A lot of women stay at Rio and they need something to do at night. Once the Chippendales show lets out, the masses start coming up the elevator.

Accessible Women: The girls travel in packs of twos and threes here, so split up your group accordingly before you make your play. The best place to meet them is on the outside balcony that's half dance floor, half observation deck, where people go to soak up a great view of the Strip.

Seating: The seating here isn't the greatest. There are seats inside the lounge, but they usually fill up quickly. On the balcony, you will find some more chairs that people rotate in and out of.

Noise: Too loud on the inside when the band is playing. The outside is perfect.

4. Dueling Piano Bar at New York–New York: Live It Up and Sing Along

Of all the dueling piano bars we've seen around the country, this one is the best. Sure, Pat O'Brien's in New Orleans invented the concept, but they don't have half the talent in the audience that this place does.

Entry: $10 minimum, and somewhat difficult after 9 p.m. due to sizable crowds. It's extremely popular, so do yourself a favor: Head over early and have a couple drinks before the craziness starts.

Party: People singing, dancing, and drinking heavily. In other words, this place is non-stop fun.

Number of Women: The single women hang out at the left in the bar area. They usually come in large groups here, so don't be afraid for your entire group of guys to go over and talk to them.

Accessible Women: Very good. Not only is everyone singing together and making fools of themselves, but people also spontaneously break out dancing in the bar area. All this allows people to let their guard down and have more fun. The girls here want to engage guys, so just go over and say hello. It's the perfect environment for your cheesiest pickup lines.

Seating: Cocktail tables on the right, bar on the left. Unless you're on a double date, stick to the left hand side.

Noise: It is loud — during some songs you are going to have to shout.

5. House of Blues at Mandalay Bay: '70s and '80s Fun.
On Thursdays, Fridays, and Saturdays, the restaurant section of House of Blues turns into a cheesy dance lounge featuring '70s disco cover bands and 80s rock cover bands.

Entry: Easy to get into but expect to pay a modest cover unless you get there during dinnertime and eat before the bands start.

Party: This turns into a fun place when the bands are playing. Compared to the other full service nightlife venues in Mandalay such as MIX, Foundation Room, and Rumjungle, you actually have a chance to get in, have fun and party.

Number of Women: A lot of girls interested in a lighter nightlife experience, not the high-class club crowd. Mandalay is a big resort, so you tend to find enough women here to give you options.

Accessible Women: Engage girls when they are going to get drinks. The bar isn't big enough to hang at, so stay in the walkway leading to the bar.

Seating: They remove a lot of seats to make space for the

dance floor, but there is seating in the back room where you can take a load off.

Noise: Not that bad. It's loud enough to keep the party going but quiet enough in the area near the bar to hold a conversation.

6. Margaritaville at Flamingo: Jimmy Buffet Always Delivers

There's no reason not to waste away for a while at this popular destination.

Entry: No entry fee, and you can walk in directly from the Strip.

Party: This place is pretty entertaining at dinnertime because there is always something going on. From constant Buffet music playing to a mermaid sliding down a water slide, Margaritaville is alive. Once 11 o'clock hits, the tables are cleared out to create a dance floor and the place gets really gets going.

Number of Women: A large number of single of women come to Margaritaville. Unfortunately, they tend to turn around and leave if they can't find a comfortable place to hang out, so you have to act quickly to convince them to stay.

Accessible Women: The bar is always packed with people sitting, but there is no place to stand around the bar to meet women. Instead, your best chance is to hang out on the perimeter of the dance floor or head upstairs to the balcony. The balcony opens up over the Strip, and you will find plenty of groups of women having a drink in the open-air environment.

Seating: Plenty of places to sit and relax. Unfortunately, most of the places to sit are away from the action.

Noise: A great environment where it is never too loud to carry on a conversation.

7. Dueling Piano Bar at Harrah's: Crowded but Worth It.

Located at the entrance to Harrah's leading to Carnival Court, the dueling piano bar gets jam-packed at night.

Entry: It's easy and free to walk in, if you can get through the crowd that is standing on the outside watching the performance.

Party: Like any dueling piano bar, the place is always alive and kicking. There aren't many people singing along and there is no place to dance, but it's still a fun, energetic environment.

Number of Women: Women tend to travel in groups of four here. They'll stay for about forty-five minutes before they start their journey to the next venue.

Accessible Women: Most of the women are sitting down at tables, but it is hard to talk to them because you'll block people's view when you go over there. The best way is to make frequent trips to the back bar and then out of the club, interacting with woman as they enter.

Seating: There are plenty of tables, but you don't want to sit at them. If you choose to sit at the tables you'll be removed from the action at the bar and will be stuck in the fairly quiet audience section watching the dueling piano performance.

Noise: It gets going, but the openness of the area keeps the sound at a great level to talk.

On the Cusp: Three Runners-Up

These three hangouts are worth considering once you've burned through the top 7.

8. The Coral Lounge at Mandalay Bay: A Good Stop for Lounge Lizards.

This is the only true lounge on the list. If you're looking for laidback, you've found it.

<u>Entry:</u> Just off the casino floor on the way to restaurant row, this casino lounge is available to everyone.

<u>Party:</u> The bands start around 9:30 p.m., and before then it's empty. The tables fill up and the dance floor gets packed around 11 p.m. The Lounge is a wide-open space, so it never quite heats up to full-boil, raging party.

<u>Number of Women:</u> In the early evening expect an older, more reserved crowd comprised of couples and some single women sitting at the tables. If you're into some type of Mrs. Robinson thing, now's your chance; otherwise, hold off until at least 10 p.m. As the evening goes on, a younger, out-to-have-fun group joins in on the dance floor. Once the place has filled up, you will find some available women, but unfortunately you're still stuck with quite a few escorted ladies.

<u>Accessible Women:</u> The pickup here is somewhat difficult because all the available women are on the dance floor. Everyone sitting is looking directly at the dance floor for entertainment, so your dance moves are on display for the whole place to see. That said, if you are willing to make an ass of yourself on the floor (we're assuming that, like most guys, you're not much of a dancer) then this place is perfect for you.

<u>Seating:</u> Plenty of seats surround the dance floor. Get there before 10 p.m. and grab a table on the far right side of the

room. From there, you can keep an eye on the dance floor and join in when needed. You don't want to sit directly on the dance floor because people dancing right in front of you will block your entire view.

Noise: Its never too loud here to carry on a conversation except when you are directly in front of the speakers on the dance floor.

9. The Beach: Off-Strip. It's always Spring Break.

This ultra-large, ultra-cheesy establishment will remind you of some place you've been before, perhaps Delaware Avenue in Philly, or Panama Beach, South Padre Island, Virginia Beach, Myrtle Beach, Cancún, Tijuana; you get the point.

Entry: Because the Beach is off-Strip, has a line, and charges a $20 cover, it ranks low in entry and access.

Party: In its heyday, the Beach was the place to party. It was notorious for its spring break feel, hot female bartenders and plenty of hard-core drinking. It has lost a bit of luster, but is still a fun atmosphere.

Number of Women: Lots of girls 21 to 25. If your group is in its 30s or older, you'll feel like the guys in Old School and will look like you're there to chaperone.

Accessible Women: When it is packed, the place is swarming with drunk guys hitting on every girl and trying to grope them on the dance floor. The best time is to go later in the night, when the girls are drunk and some of the meatheads have cleared out. It may be down to lady leftovers by then, but they are in a mood to hook up. But face it, this place will make you feel well past your prime.

Seating: No real place to sit down. This place is big, so your group will probably end up separated from one another once you walk in the door. Use the bar to the immediate right of the entrance as your rendezvous point because it's so loud, you can't count on using your cell phone to find your way back.

Noise: Super loud when you are close to the dance floor. If you want to talk and just hang out, then head upstairs to the balcony and poolroom area.

10. Cleopatra's Barge at Caesars Palace: Worth a Look-See

Although it's easy to get to, Cleopatra's isn't always your best option. However, it can be pretty good at times and is worth poking your head in as you walk through the casino.

Entry: Easy and simple entry from the casino floor.

Party: When the music gets going and the theatrical smoke is pumping, it can turn into a fun place.

Number of Women: It is a small place and has a bit of an older crowd, so the number of available women is low, but they are there.

Accessible Women: Get ready to act as the boy toy for an older, divorced mom. If you are up for that, then you won't have too much trouble. Think of it as the place where the moms of the girls from the Beach cut loose.

Seating: There are a few tables around the barge. You can score a good one if you get there early enough. Other than that, expect to stand while you drink. If your group is large, this is not a good option.

Noise: Conversations are difficult when the music is pumping. Make your way to the side casino bar to get away from the noise.

> ## The Lost-and-Found Tour
>
> Many of these venues are lined up next to one another, making for one large, roving party. You'll find that many groups of girls wander from one place to another, searching for a good time. Use this to your advantage. Say hello to a girl when you are leaving one venue. When you see her again, use the line "Didn't I see you at . . ." It gives you a reason to talk to her and you are not an unknown to her anymore.

🚗 TRAVELING AT NIGHT

Even though the hotels are right next to one another, the Strip is bigger than you think. It's important to choose the proper mode of transportation before you start off for the night.

Walking

If you made the smart accommodations choice, you won't have to travel far to find a nighttime venue. Choose places within walking distance of your hotel. Again, several of the best nighttime options are right next to one another, so you don't really have to rely on anything more than your Chuck Taylors to get you from one place to the next. And, oh yeah: Never, ever wear your Chucks out on the town at night.

Taxis

If you have to go a distance, perhaps a cab is your best bet. Here are a few important Vegas taxi reminders.

1. Five is the limit. Don't try to get more than five people into a cab, or you're asking for problems.

2. You have to get them at the taxi stand of a property. Remember, this isn't New York: You can't yell "Yo!" from the middle of the street and expect the cab to pick you up. In fact,

there's a good chance they'll run you over, you drunken nut.

3. Expect the strip club sell. The second you get in, the driver will be all over you to head to a strip club so they can get a generous kickback. Even if your destination is a strip club, do your homework and avoid the place the cabbie "recommends": he's only interested in making a buck, not making sure you get exactly what you want.

4. If it's the weekend, expect it to take a while to get a cab. The lines can get especially long as the shows let out. This is something you should always consider when you choose to venture off of the Strip.

Limos

A limo is the key to the kingdom. If you want to do Vegas right, you've got to buck up, but it's well worth the investment.

♣ Book the Whole Night:

A limo is an experience: It makes you top dog and lets you travel in style, so charter a limo for the whole night. You don't want to feel like Cinderella when the clock strikes 12 and the driver kicks you out of the backseat.

♣ They're Everywhere:

Limos are easier to get in Vegas than water. There are more limos per capita in Las Vegas than anywhere in the world. Just call a limo company and request one: The standard hourly rate is $35/hour plus tip. The tip should depend on how much the driver hooked you up, but 15 to 20 percent is average.

♣ Think of the Savings:

$35 well spent. Just the first round of drinks you drink in the limo as opposed to at the bar will save you the $35 for the hour. Think of the limo as your rolling bar.

♣ Get Liquored Up:

Make sure you get liquor and beer as soon as you get in the limo. Don't waste your time stocking up before you get in — just make the liquor store your first stop. Tell the driver you need to load up and get you where you need to go.

♣ Fuggetaboudit:

Don't worry if on one of your stops you decide to kick it around in the casino for a couple of hours while the meter is running on the limo. Just the fact that you could easily go to any place in two seconds is worth it. Besides, once you defray the cost across your entire group, this luxury isn't setting you back too much.

♣ Call Ahead and Get the Right Size:

Just like everything else in town, it pays to think ahead. Although they're everywhere, you'd be surprised at just how hard it can be to find a limo on a fight night or pretty much on any weekend. When purchasing the limo, be sure to let them know your group size. A basic limo seats six, a

---

$$$ IF MONEY IS NO OBJECT

The Party Bus: A party bus is like a roving nightclub that fits sixteen. You and your crew can crank the music, stand up and move around, dance, and party like rock stars. Party buses get reserved weeks in advance and cost four times the amount of normal limos, but it is worth it if your group is big and you have women hitting the town with you.

---

stretch limo seats eight, and a super stretch limo seats ten. Any bigger, and you have to go for a Limo Bus, which seats sixteen, or an Limo Escalade, which seats twenty.

Using Limos to Pick Up Women

Girls are fascinated by limos. They feel like they are princesses when they are inside of them. Most girls who visit Vegas haven't been in a limo since their prom, so if you do end up giving a girl a ride, she'll be impressed.

Limos also serve as a great place to hook up. The limo offers a hookup sanctuary that is quick to get to, and you don't have to spend the night. Just get a girl in the limo for a ride down the Strip and a glass of champagne, and the likelihood of getting some action will increase tenfold. She'll feel safe in the limo, and she'll also feel like she's doing something fun and slightly naughty.

When you guys stop off to get a drink and encounter a group of ladies, an offer to head off to another local hot spot in your waiting limo has a lot of appeal — use it your best advantage.

Classic Vegas Mistake

Getting a Limo from a Hotel: Although charting a limo from a limo company is a good idea, don't make the mistake of grabbing a hotel limo. These limos are basically just like taxis, and they are going to take you to your destination without any of the benefits of having a limo in the first place. On top of that, you can end up paying $50 for the same taxi ride that would have cost you $10. Charter a limo only from a limo company.

 # SHOWS IN VEGAS

There are all types of shows in Vegas, but not all of them make sense for a group of guys. Allow us to point you in the right direction.

Why Go to a Show

We know what you're thinking: Shows are where the women go when the men are out gambling, right? Wrong. There are plenty that will appeal to your group and it is a great way to spend a couple of hours. Plus, at the very least you're in a room full of unescorted women!

Three Reasons to Hit a Show

1. <u>They Made for a Good Night Out.</u> Although everything else you do in Vegas can be done at any hour, shows are only available at night. A good show is a great way to really hit the town. It's a perfect event to plan your evening around. Follow it up with a late dinner and some drinks and you've got yourself a good evening.

2. <u>Old-School Vegas.</u> A big show is one of the staples of a trip to Vegas. Everyone knows about the Vegas shows, and the Vegas showgirls. If you want to feel like a Vegas Rat Packer, you have to take the time to take in a show.

3. <u>Women.</u> You may meet some women at a show, and then again later at the nearest bar. You will have a common experience to share, so chat 'em up. It is a great icebreaker.

Purchasing Show Tickets

Buy Tickets Before You Get to Vegas

To keep the group together, it would be good to go ahead and buy show tickets before you arrive to Vegas. It can be hard to get buy-in from the guys on going to a show once they get a taste of the booze and the tables when they hit town. Get them to commit in advance; otherwise, you'll get a handful of naysayers once you touch down in town. Plus, if you wait until the last minute, the only shows you'll be able to get tickets to are the ones you wouldn't want to see, anyway.

Are Shows Too Expensive?

Shows seem expensive, but they are worth the experience. $85 might seem like a lot to pony up for a show, but that $85 will provide a lasting memory of your time in Vegas. You can easily blow that type of cash in a fraction of the time in the casino or at a bar.

What to Do If You Didn't Think Ahead

If you didn't think ahead, you have a couple of options to get decent deals on day-of tickets:

* **Tickets2Nite:** This place offers half-price tickets on the day of the show. You'll find this place behind the giant Coke bottle next to the MGM Grand. It opens at noon daily.

❖ **Tix4Tonight:** Also offering half-price tickets, Tix4Tonight has three locations: next to the Harley-Davidson Café; the Strip entrance to the Fashion Show Mall; and across from the Stardust on the Strip.

Unfortunately, since these are always day-of show tickets there's probably not a very good chance that you'll be able to get a large block right next to one another. So your group will most likely have to split up for the show.

🍸 Classic Vegas Mistake

The Show Stand-By Line: Many show box offices have a line for people who don't have tickets but are waiting for others not to show up to get into the show. There are three reasons why you don't want to do this. First, people start lining up hours before the show. You don't want to waste your time standing around when there is so much to do in Vegas. Second, there are very few people who actually get in, so all that time in line was a waste. Finally, they won't let you in until after the first break in the show. So you'll miss a quarter of the show and have to disturb the audience in your row as you get to your seat. Either buy tickets beforehand or find something else to do.

 ### *THE LITTLE BLACK BOOK*'S LUCKY 7 SHOWS FOR GROUPS OF GUYS

1. Blue Man Group: The Ultimate in Sensory Overload.

Three blue men doing strange things: You won't understand the concept of this show until you see it for yourself. Trust us, these guys are much less annoying in person than they are on those Intel commercials.

Cost: Ranges from $70 to $90, depending on the time of year.

Availability: Two shows a day and in a big show room, but an extremely popular show. Buy tickets at least a couple of days out.

2. Penn & Teller: Magic that works.

These comedians of magic won't bore you with cheesy stage magic like the other magicians on the Strip.

Cost: $75

Availability: You can usually get tickets the day of the show. The venue is extremely large for a show of this magnitude.

3. The Amazing Jonathan: A Rude Blend of Magic and Comedy.

The Amazing Jonathan is an almost disturbing display of dark humor. The Amazing Jonathan takes comedy to his own alarming level.

Cost: Ranges from $55 to $65

Availability: He does two shows a day, and tickets aren't too hard to come by. If you want to sit close to the stage, then purchase beforehand. But since the venue is small, there is not a bad seat in the house.

4. Various Headline Comedians.

Vegas always features some of the best stand-up comics in the business. Regulars include huge names like Jerry Seinfeld, Chris Rock, and Ray Romano; their shows aren't cheap to go to at all. Other names like Lewis Black, Dave Attell, and Dane Cook might be a bit more affordable. Comedy shows are a great place to keep the drinks flowing.

Cost: Ranges from $30 to $100

Headline comedians usually do a three-day run of shows in Vegas and they tend to sell out a couple of weeks in advance. You don't always know who is going to be performing when you are in Vegas, so you need to do some online research beforehand.

5) *Mystère*: If you must see a Cirque du Soleil Show.

Of all the Cirque shows, *Mystère* is the only one recommended for a group of guys. It's much less intense than some of the others, and its proximity to a good post-show party place doesn't hurt.

Cost: Ranges from $60 to $95

Availability: Buy tickets at least a couple of weeks in advance, since while the show has been around for a while, it still is extremely popular.

6. Wayne Newton: Mr. Las Vegas Himself

I know this sounds bad, but Wayne is an experience that everybody must have once. He didn't get the title Mr. Las Vegas by accident — he earned it by putting on a damn good show.

Cost: Ranges from $75 and up, depending on venue.

Availability: If it's a weekend, you should probably get a ticket a couple days before or you will be sitting in the nosebleed section.

7. Tournament of Kings.

You probably think this show is for kids only, but you'd be wrong. While the notion of knights riding around jousting with one another may seem pretty silly, the fun atmosphere and energetic environment makes up for it. This is also the only show that comes with dinner, but be prepared to use your hands, because utensils are not supplied.

<u>Cost:</u> $50

<u>Availability:</u> There usually is open space in this show, so you can call the day of for tickets.

Word-of-Mouth Wonders:

Wayne Newton certainly has a reputation that extends beyond Vegas, but there are other entertainers in town who don't. Once you arrive, you'll be bombarded with promotions for expensive shows headlined by people you've probably never heard of. We're not saying don't go, because most of these folks are really talented. Amazingly, Danny Gans and Clint Holmes, two people who aren't household names, pack them in every night.

Topless Shows

Topless shows are a good way to get the group in the partying mood, especially when the group doesn't know what to do. Topless shows are the epitome of Vegas, and when you see one, you know that you are really experiencing the town. One of the only minuses is that the shows usually start later in the evening.

Topless Show Recommendations

1. <u>La Femme</u> at the MGM: This show is famous because it actually started at The Crazy Horse in Paris (not to be confused with The Crazy Horse Too). It's an upbeat, exotic show.

2. <u>Crazy Girls</u> at the Rivera. This show is fairly interactive: The dancers work their way into the crowd.

3. <u>Skintight</u> at Harrah's: Skintight features a lot of topless dancers and, inexplicably, a male lead singer. If you can ignore the fact that there's a dude up there, too, the women are hot.

4. <u>Midnight Fantasy</u> at the Luxor: You might be surprised to learn that this show doesn't actually start at midnight; shows are at 8:30 and 10 p.m.

5. _Bite at the Stratosphere_: The ultimate in topless cheese. These sexy vixens have fangs. You will find this show both amusing and erotic in equal measure.

LATE NIGHT

Las Vegas is not what you think during the wee hours of the morning. Yes, everything in Vegas is 24 hours, but the people aren't. A fair number of people vacationing here are from the East Coast, and they will get tired as the night wears on. Especially on their first day, when they are still on East Coast time. Your options are limited.

Late Night Partying

After 3 a.m., your options are limited to casino bars to drink. Unfortunately, there is nothing more boring than sitting at a casino bar at 4 in the morning.

Late Night Partying Options

1. After-Hours Clubs. Avoid even trying to go to after-hours places like Drai's at Barbary Coast. You will pay a hefty sum — and that's even if they let you in. This is a club crowd, not a drink-and-carousec rowd; you just won't fit in.

2. The Casino Bar. A boring casino video poker bar will be one of your only choices inside the casinos. Not only are these bars dead during the late night, the only women around will be those of the working type. Expect to be solicited multiple times.

3. Strip Clubs. While most of the good dancers will already by gone by this time, some clubs like Crazy Horse Too keep the party going until the daylight hours. Whether it is worth the

effort to leave the Strip and venture back out the to strip clubs at this hour is up to you.

4. <u>Gaming.</u> Gambling is the best option during the late night. While the gaming crowd at this hour is a bit strange and usually drunk, you are pretty much guaranteed that something unusual will happen that you can tell a story about later. Just be careful that you don't get too drunk and end up being the story yourself.

Sleeping

If you are doing something and you are not going full steam with it, then you should bail and get some sleep. Sleep will recharge you for some good times the next day, while your buddies who pull the all-nighter will be zombies all day.

Sleeping

1. <u>Don't stay up just to stay up</u>. If you have hit the wall and are just staying up to stay up, then bail and hit the sheets. You will be able to get some good sleep and be awake in the morning, sitting by the pool while your buddies are still passed out from the night before.

2. <u>Sleeping is free</u>. In Vegas, sleeping is one of the only available blocks of time when you won't be spending any money. Take advantage of it.

> ### ℸ Classic Vegas Mistake
>
> **Venturing out by yourself:** Use the buddy system. Don't wander off on your own. One of the biggest mistakes a group makes is that a person will wander off and you lose them for the night. You usually won't be able to find your group; it's hard to spot someone in a crowed casino. You will end up being lost, just wandering around trying to find your way back.

Putting It All Together

Now that you know what your options are, it's time to get out and hit the town. Remember, there are too many cool things to do at night in Sin City to stay at any one place for too long. A good night out in Las Vegas means hitting a few different stops along the way. Go to a show, get a limo, hit a few bars and have a good time. I'm sure by this point you're thinking that we've overlooked what is probably the signature nighttime Las Vegas activity for groups of guys: the gentlemen's club. Don't worry, we've got you covered with an entire chapter devoted to those magical places where guys really like to spend money in Vegas.

✶ Chapter 9 ✶

Gentlemen's Clubs:
Gentlemen, Start Your Spending

✶ ....

Ah, nighttime in Sin City. It's the heart of the evening: You've done the big dinner, the bars, the gambling, and now it's time for what really makes Las Vegas unique — the gentlemen's clubs. Sure, we know there are some dingy little strip joints back in your hometown, and almost every big city has one or more "up-scale" gentlemen's club, but they don't hold a candle to what's going on in Las Vegas. Back at home, a visit to a strip club is almost invariably a furtive, disappointing experience. About the best you can say for it is that you don't do it very often. We guarantee that if this is your first trip to Sin City, you're probably not prepared for what you're about to see. Unlike most towns that hide their topless bars, Vegas flaunts them. So step inside. You've got a truly great night out with the guys in store for you.

 LAS VEGAS GENTLEMEN'S CLUBS

Vegas gentlemen's clubs have women. Lots of women. Lots of hot women who will flirt with you; lots of hot women who will flirt with you and then take their clothes off for you. Can you — a simple man raised on the beautiful dream of MTV dancers, Penthouse Pets and Victoria's Secret models, but without the hope of ever actually meeting one — possibly ask for anything more? We thought not.

A Party Like No Other

How many times have you been to a dance club or concert and not been able to take your eyes off the go-go dancers? They catch your attention. There they are, above everyone else, hot women with barely any clothes on. You can't keep your eyes off them. At a gentlemen's club, those girls are everywhere. They are the reason the club exists, and the reason you're sitting there with your mouth open.

A night in the gentlemen's club is the same as the best party that you could ever imagine throwing at your house. Naked women are all around you, dancing and partying. Face it, the things that happen here will never happen at your house, and even if they did, the girls wouldn't be nearly as attractive and your neighbors would call the cops. So head to a gentlemen's club, where the girls will knock your socks off and you don't have to spend much for a great time (although you can if you really want to).

Vegas: The Home of Strip Joint Respectability

In most other towns, polite society frowns upon the frequenting of gentlemen's clubs in much the same way it frowns upon other unseemly acts. Drunkenness, public urination, loud and lewd comments shouted from a passing car: These are actually preferable, in the minds of some, to going to look at naked women dancing for your pleasure. You feel so guilty for going that it's usually difficult to even recruit a crew of guys to go with you. Everyone has to invent an alibi to serve up to his significant other, as the mere mention of a gentlemen's club around most women is enough to brand you as a Class 3 sex offender or worse, and make you feel like a complete pervert

In Vegas, however, an evening out at a gentlemen's club is, well, gentlemanly. It is an accepted, expected, even respected form of entertainment that carries no more moral weight or stigma than going to an ice-cream parlor — or better, actually: strip clubs aren't fattening. After all, in the city that runs on 24-hour booze and gambling, what harm is there in cultivating the company of beautiful, naked women? It's the same as going to a bar. A gentlemen's club is a delightful place to sit and relax with your friends over a few drinks. The drink prices are similar or just as cheap as those at the bars and clubs that people go to everyday, with the added bonus of being surrounded on all sides by beautiful, naked women. Finally, everyone expects that when you head home you'll have some strip joint stories to tell, so you might as well hit the town and come up with a few.

Night Clubs Versus Gentlemen's Clubs

Some faction of your group will want to go to a nightclub rather than a gentlemen's club. These people must be hunted down and ruthlessly suppressed. The nightclub proponents will say, "Let's go to a club where we have a chance to pick up some women!" On the surface, this is a reasonable position, but here's the truth: Your group is going to have a much better time at the gentlemen's club. Here are a few reasons why.

Why a Gentlemen's Club is Better than a Night Club

No Wait: A nightclub is extremely difficult for a group of guys to get into; remember, they want a 4:1 ratio of women to guys. Gentlemen's clubs are easy to get into because they want you in the door.

Lower Door Costs: A gentlemen's club is nominally $20 a head (but often free), whereas at a nightclub you might need to tip the velvet rope man as much as a $100 to get in the door.

Better Girls: At a nightclub, girls have no incentive to talk to you. A group of guys looking for action is about as attractive to your basic anorexic, champagne-quaffing nightclub waif as a herd of wild hogs. At a gentlemen's club, beautiful naked girls will seek you out and strike up a conversation.

Not as Loud: Nightclubs are loud. This is because their main function is to keep women dancing, and to keep you buying them drinks. You have to shout in someone's ear to be heard, because they don't want you to be heard. At a gentlemen's club, the music is set at an enjoyable level that is not too loud. They want conversation because the girls need to talk to you to buy lap dances.

<u>Better Atmosphere:</u> Nightclubs are crowed places. They pack people in like sardines because they want a full dance floor. You have to fight your way up to the bar just to get a drink. Gentlemen's clubs can get crowded, too, but are usually larger, have lots of seating, multiple bars, and plenty of attractive cocktail servers circling endlessly to bring you drinks.

<u>Lower Drink Prices:</u> Drinks can cost upward of $14 for a Red Bull Vodka at a nightclub; drink prices at a gentlemen's clubs are around $7 to $10.

<u>Easy to Get a Table:</u> Tables need to be reserved and will set you back at least $300 at a nightclub. At a gentlemen's club, tables are available to everyone, with no bottle minimums.

👄 GENTLEMEN'S CLUBS LAYOUTS

You need to become familiar with the basic layout of the Las Vegas clubs before you venture inside. If you don't, you might end up in the wrong section, where dances are twice as expensive. Clubs are made up of six sections.

The Entryway

Once you enter through the doors, you will be confronted by a bouncer to check your IDs, and then by a booth where a pretty cashier will take your entry fee. There is a chance you will have your entry fee waived if you tell the bouncer that you drove or walked, and did not take a taxi. He might let you in for free.

Food at Gentlemen's Clubs

More gentlemen's clubs are offering food selections. Ranging from appetizers to sandwiches to steaks, the food in these places is low cost and not bad. If a club does not offer food, it usually allows for delivery from a pizza joint. Just casually let it slip to your friends back home that you had a pizza delivered to your table in a gentlemen's club, then sit back and accept their awe and adulation. Also, many of the clubs have strawberries, chocolate, and whipped cream on the menu. This is a strategically cool thing to order if you have a good party going with a group of strippers at your table. Can you imagine a hot stripper on your lap, seductively licking whipped cream off of a strawberry?

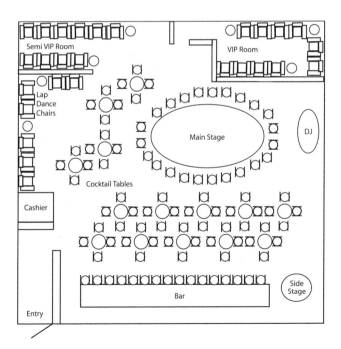

Tipping the Doorman

Some clubs have a doorman past the cashier, near the entrance, who will seat you. You don't have to tip these guys unless they really go out of their way to help you, by pushing tables together, finding chairs, etc. The best strategy is to politely decline their help by telling them you're heading for the bar. If the club is so packed that there's no room near the bar, it may be a good sign that you should take your business elsewhere.

Your New Pal, the Bathroom Attendant:

These days, pretty much every place has a bathroom attendant, so if you have to hit the head (and you will), make sure you have an extra single with you. Apparently, the bathroom attendant is just another stage in the strip club's attempt to be classy. They will offer you liquid soap when you wash your hands and a towel when you dry. They have an array of musk and cologne products to offer, as well as breath mints and mouthwash. Centered prominently amid this bounty is his tip basket. An interesting variation on the theme is the wisecracking bathroom attendant. The wisecracker is a character type that many places employ. A lot of guys try to get out of the bathroom without leaving a tip, so the wisecracker attempts to rope them in with a few raunchy one-liners. It usually prompts a smile and a tip. So, if you're in the market for a few dirty jokes, you'll find them, as usual, in the bathroom; surprisingly, they're not written on the stalls.

The Bar

The bar is a great place to get a drink where you won't be pressured into getting a lap dance. You can start here when you first walk in to give yourself a chance to get a feel for the club; and likewise after you've been at it for a while and feel like you need a break from the constant attention of beautiful, naked women.

Many clubs have televisions with sports on them, so you can catch a game that you have some money riding on. If the club is crowded and all the cocktail tables are full, sit at the bar and wait. If you see a group that is about to leave, sit down immediately before a doorman puts a reserved sign on it so he can score a tip.

The Stage

The stage is the center of the club, where the main action is, and where much of your attention will be focused. A seat at one of the chairs surrounding the stage gives you an up close and personal view of the featured stage dancer(s). You must tip while you are sitting at the stage, so be sure to have some $1 bills ready. Some of your larger clubs may have several stages.

Cocktail Tables

The clubs are filled with these tables. Four rolling chairs surround each of the small cocktail tables. This is the best place to sit with a group to hang out and wait for the dancers to approach. If your group is bigger than four, push these tables together so you can form a large circle.

☐ Classic Vegas Mistake

The Wrong Person in the Point Position: When you sit at a table, there will always be one chair that is more accessible to the dancers and the walkways than the others. The position is referred to as the "point position." Whoever sits here will be the one that 80 percent of the dancers will approach first. You must take care that your point man here is a smooth-talking partier. There is nothing worse for somebody who wants a dance to be stuck far down the table while his incompetent point man is sending all the dancers away and giving your table a bad rep. Choose wisely, or suffer.

The Lap Dance Chairs

These chairs are bigger and more stable than the cocktail chairs. They line the outskirts of the room. Dancers prefer to give dances here because they don't have to worry about the chair rolling around when they are dancing. Don't sit in these chairs if you don't intend to get a lap dance. They won't make a good place for conversation with your buddies, the girls will get irritated that you are monopolizing their money chairs, and the bouncers will make you leave.

Semi-VIP Rooms

The semi-VIP room is a place for a more intimate dance. The semi-VIP rates are either $30 a dance or $100 for four, depending on the club. This "room" is an area sectioned off from the main floor, but is not actually a private room. Lap dances are a little better here because it is more private than out on the main floor, but you have to be continuously buying dances to stay.

VIP Rooms

This VIP room is a completely separate room from the main floor, with its own entrance, bouncer, and rules governing its use. The VIP room rate is based upon the hour. The usual fee is $400 per hour, plus bottle service for you and the girl at around $150. On top of that, the bouncer is usually pressuring you to give him a tip. Only go back here if you really like the dancer and you have some money to burn.

CHOOSING A GENTLEMEN'S CLUB

Las Vegas is the Mecca of gentlemen's clubs. With so many to choose from, it is easy to get lost and just assume that every club is the same. Clubs vary in many different ways, and as always, it's important that you pick a club that meets the needs of your group.

♦ Classic Vegas Mistake

Being Lured into VIP Rooms: A stripper's objective is to get you to the VIP room. She will sell you on a better and more personal dance in VIP. She really just wants it because it will be better money for her time spent. When you are in there, the girl knows she has your money whether she dances or not, so she will proceed to drink and engage you in conversation to burn through the hour. In addition, all clubs have rules governing physical contact between guys and strippers, whether in the VIP room or out, and generally speaking, you are not going to get much more here than you would in a lap dance chair. VIP rooms do not maximize your gentlemen's club experience, but instead shorten it because you blow through your money faster. In other words, VIP rooms are not worth it.

What Makes a Good Club

Clubs can be ranked based on six key factors. The higher the rating on each of the factors, the better the club.

Clubs Criteria

Quality of Dancers: The dancers need to be hot and sexy.

Quality of Lap Dances: The girls need to know how to give a good lap dance. What's a "good" lap dance? You'll know one when you get one! This is what you are here for.

Number of Dancers: A club needs enough dancers so you can get a dance when you want from a dancer you want.

Atmosphere: A good club atmosphere is one where you feel like you are at a big party. Both the employees and the clientele need to be comfortable and having a good time.

Management: Management can be a deciding factor in the way you feel about the club. Do they give you a hard time getting in the door? Do they give you a hard time getting a seat? Do they make you move if you are not slamming drinks? Do they enforce rules that the dancers can't give good dances?

Establishment: The establishment is the physical plant of the club. Some clubs have plenty of rooms and seats, while other are tight arrangements. Also, the club needs to be clean and well kept; otherwise you will feel you are at a truck stop peep show.

CHOOSING A CLUB
Club Rankings

	Dancers	Dances	Number	Atmosphere	Management	Establishment	TOTALS
Spearmint Rhino	9	7	10	10	8	10	54
Crazy Horse Too	8	10	9	10	7	7	51
Striptease	5	10	4	10	10	9	48
Club Paradise	10	7	7	8	6	9	47
Treasure's	7	7	6	9	7	10	46
Sapphires	7	7	8	7	7	9	45
Jaguar's	8	7	6	7	7	9	44
Cheetah's	7	9	7	6	8	6	43
Olympic Gardens	6	7	9	7	7	6	42
Glitter Gulch	4	6	4	6	6	6	32

1. Spearmint Rhino: Simply the Best.

The Rhino blows the competition away. The only downside to this club is that it is so popular, it is sometimes hard to find a place to sit on weekends.

Dancers: Almost perfect. They have the best dancers in town, but they also have a large group of not so good dancers who end up taking up some of your time.

Dances: Strong, but could be better. Given the club's popularity, the girls are always able to find a customer, making it more of a seller's market.

Number of Dancers: This place is packed with dancers every night of the week. The mix is half local dancers and half dancers in town for a couple of days.

Atmosphere: Ridiculously good. You'll feel like you just walked into a Roman orgy. Sometimes they have five to six girls onstage at once. There are smaller stages in the auxiliary sections, which are only open when the place is busy, which is very often. The best place to sit is in the main room on the raised section on the left. These tables won't have people walking in front of and around your table, so it offers a little more privacy while keeping a view of the entire club and the stage.

Management: They have solid customer service and don't make you move if you are nursing your drink. The floor men do expect to be tipped if they give you a table. The cocktail servers are plentiful and very friendly. The management here wants to keep an upscale environment, so the place is remarkably clean and well kept.

<u>Establishment:</u> Newly remodeled, the Rhino has an upscale feel to it. When you walk through the doors, there is a room to your left with a small stage and a bar that is only open at night. The main floor has a large main stage with cocktail tables surrounding it, and the newly added back room has two smaller stages but has a blocked view of the main stage.

2. Crazy Horse Too: The Horse Gallops 24 Hours a Day

Once the reigning champ, Crazy Horse Too was upstaged when the Rhino expanded. Still, the place is a pure party and the girls are amazing. This is the only club in town that has good dancers all day long. Located next to the Sahara and I-15, it is difficult to find if you are driving here. Stay in the right lane on Sahara when you leave the Strip going west, and make a right before the first underpass. The road will wind around and drop you off right in front of Crazy Horse.

<u>Dancers:</u> A solid group of beautiful dancers work here. These girls are out to make money so they can be very aggressive. Sometimes they sit on your lap and refuse to move if you don't buy them a dance. You may expect to be approached by many dancers here over the course of an evening, and you may become annoyed having to keep turning down dancer after beautiful dancer. Deal with it.

<u>Dances:</u> Dances are great here. If you get a dance, move over to the bigger chairs against the back wall. It is a little darker and more intimate, and the dancers are free to give you a better dance because the chairs are not moving around.

<u>Number of Dancers:</u> The Horse has a large group of dancers working 24 hours a day. More than any other club, you will be able to find dancers here during the happy hour and late-night times.

<u>Atmosphere:</u> Crazy Horse Too falls in the middle of the pack.

Your fellow customers will range from a business executive to a construction worker. The music during the day is rock music, and they tend to play long songs, which can be a nice change of pace, as most clubs seem to blare hip-hop all the time.

<u>Management:</u> Think old-school Vegas on this one. Expect to pay entry at the door, as it is hard to talk your way though here. When this place is packed and there is a line outside, you may want to tip the doorman to jump the line.

<u>Establishment:</u> A small but intimate place. From the exterior, the place seems a little on the shady side, but when you walk through the doors you will find it very comfortable. Plasma TVs are in the corners, making it a great place to watch sports. Drink prices are a little on the expensive side, so if you want to save a few bucks for more dances, stick with the domestic bottled beer.

$$$ IF MONEY IS NO OBJECT

The Key to the Crazy Horse Back Door: The ultimate spender at Crazy Horse Too is awarded with a coveted prize: a key to the back door of the Crazy Horse, where you enter directly into the VIP room. There are only a handful of keys out there, and if you want to get one, expect to blow a boatload of money on women and booze. We are talking tens of thousands of dollars. But once you get a key, it is yours for life and you will be part of a prestige membership of supreme gentlemen club connoisseurs.

---

3. Striptease: Take the Good with the Bad

Striptease is small and intimate, but usually fairly empty. On weekends, a really first-class group of hot dancers work Striptease, and the club takes off into a full-out party.

Dancers: The dancers here are in the mood to have a good time. They know they are going to make some money, but they are not cash hounds. This is the only club where the girls will sit with you without the pressure of getting a lap dance immediately. The quality of dancers ranges from average to incredible, so you can find some true diamonds in the rough.

Dances: Incredible. Without question you get the best value for your lap dance dollar here. The best place to get one in the main room is on the couches on the backside of the bar, or on the smaller couches located in the nook behind the DJ stand.

Number of Dancers: There are not that many dancers here before 10 p.m. This is a smaller club, so you will never have the mass of girls like at Spearmint Rhino or Sapphires. But, the upside is that the crowd is small, too, creating a favorable dancer-to-guy ratio.

Atmosphere: An energetic, non intimidating atmosphere. The music is fun, never too much hip hop or dance music. Unlike other clubs, you will still find here the old gentlemen's club traditions like the bachelor being embarrassed onstage, shot specials, shower shows, and a couple songs of half price lap dances.

Management: Management is very friendly and accommodating. They appreciate your business. You won't get the same cocky attitude that you find at other clubs, since this place is underutilized and they are still searching for new business.

Establishment: A rather small place. When you walk in, there is a bar to your right that is a great place to hang out and get your bearings on the club. You can still see the dancers because the main stage forms the top of the bar. The main floor is elevated and is comprised of plenty of cocktail tables to grab a seat.

4. Club Paradise: High Class in Its Own Way

In its heyday, Club Paradise was the best, most luxurious club in town. Located across the street from the Hard Rock, Paradise opens at 5 p.m. There is no self-parking, so if you drive, be ready to valet or to park at the Hard Rock and walk there.

Dancers: Every girl at Paradise must go through an audition process to become a dancer. They choose only beautiful girls who have the right attitude to work here, so any dancer you choose will be a good selection.

Dances: Dances are average. Dressed in gowns, the girls are extremely hot so they don't have to give the hard lap dances to keep your business. They do pressure you to pay the extra money and go into the VIP room, where they promise the dances will be more intimate, which they rarely are.

Number of Dancers: Around 9 p.m., the place gets stocked with plenty of dancers, but before that, it's a bit thin.

Atmosphere: A high-class, chill atmosphere with good music. A great place to spend the early evening and have some drinks and some entertainment. Contributing to the atmosphere are the "shot girls." These girls give you a half a lap dance and a test-tube shot taken from their breast or mouth for $10. It is a great way to buy a drink for a buddy who is unsure about getting a lap dance.

Management: They used to be tough around here, but with the fierce competition they have established better customer service. Expect to pay a tip when the doorman shows you to a table.

Establishment: This is the one club that does not have a Stripper pole on the stage. This doesn't sound like much, but the effect is to make you feel like you are at a high-class house party rather than a club. When getting a table, get one on the right-hand side of the room against the wall with the mirrors. There is less foot traffic here than in the rest of the club. Paradise offers a wine list of good breadth and depth — surprising in any strip club, where seven out of ten guys stick to beer, and the rest to shots. Again, if you want to save your money for the lap honeys, bypass the wine list.

5. Treasures: Eat, Drink, and Be Danced On
A newly built palace, this is the only club in town that features a fine dining restaurant and a great buffet.

<u>Dancers:</u> Average dancers, with a couple hotties and not-so-hotties sprinkled in.

<u>Dances:</u> They give good dances here, but some girls won't get into them if you get a dance smack in the middle of the room.

<u>Number of Dancers:</u> Treasures is building a good team of dancers, but still doesn't compete with the other clubs in numbers. A lot of dancers in town from California work Treasures on the weekends.

<u>Atmosphere:</u> A friendly, upscale environment. The girls aren't in a party mood, they are here to make money, so you should expect to hear, "Do you want a dance?" very often.

<u>Management:</u> One of the more progressive management groups, Treasure's is big into VIP hosting and establishing relationships. You may want to call ahead, ask for the manager, and let him know you are coming. That way, he will meet you at the door and have a group of seats waiting for you.

<u>Establishment:</u> When you walk in the front door, the gourmet restaurant is located directly to your left. The club consists of two levels, but we recommend staying on the bottom floor

unless you want to go into the VIP room. In the main room, the buffet is on the left and the main bar is on the right. The bar is not a good place to sit, because you will be facing away from the main stage. The best tables are the ones in the far right front of the room because they are a bit more secluded than the rest, with good sight lines.

6. Sapphires: Too Big for Its Own Good

Welcome to the largest strip club in the world. In this case, however, the biggest does not mean the best.

Dancers: Every shape, size, and species of dancer works here. There are so many dancers to choose from that you will be able to find one who works for you, and probably many more than one, but it may take a little while to weed through the crowd.

Dances: There are some dancers here who will work the lap dance pretty hard for you, but most of the time they tend to be pretty tame.

Number of Dancers: Hundreds of dancers work here on any given weekend. Most are from California, in town for the weekend to make some money. Sapphires is the place where porn stars showcase themselves in Vegas, but it is tough to get a dance from them because they usually already have the whole night booked in VIP.

Atmosphere: You will be reminded of your gentlemen's club back home, where it is all about the money. The dancers here won't hang with you. They just want to make some money and be on their way. Because Sapphires has done a great job promoting the club, the huge hangar-like space will literally be packed wall to wall with guys trying to find a seat.

Management: Management wants to pack in the masses here,

and they do a fairly decent job. The place is maintained and remains remarkably clean given the volume of traffic.

Establishment: The place is one huge warehouse with stages. It is difficult to see the dancers on the stage because the backdrop wall is made up of hundreds of colored LEDs that never let your eyes adjust. Try sitting at the bar on the far end of the big room near the bathrooms. It is more of a chill crowd of dancers here, and you can get drinks faster.

Why are there differences in dances at the clubs?

Dancers work off of supply and demand. If they know they have a line of guys willing to buy a dance from them, then they have no big incentive to try to impress you with a good dance in hopes that you will buy another. On the other hand, if there are not a lot of guys buying dances, then the dancer will make it worth your while and try to monopolize you with multiple dances.

7. Jaguar's: If Only the Girls Would Show

The building is amazing, the club is upscale, the dancers are hot; they just need more of them to compete with the other clubs.

Dancers: Very good. It seems like a lot of sexy dancers all decided to work at the same place. There are some uglies, but overall, Jaguar's is able to keep the hot ones.

Dances: The dances are good here. The chair's arms are too high, so the dancer will be limited in the number of positions that she can dance for you. If you are going to get a dance, head to the left or right walls that are lined with couches.

Number of Dancers: They could use many more. The best

girls get monopolized quickly, leaving you with the rest of the litter.

Atmosphere: Since the room is so big, if it is not crowded you will feel like you are missing the party and want to head somewhere else. The center stage is dark and oddly shaped, so there is not much entertainment to keep your eyes focused on. The clientele is more of a convention crowd rather than a party crowd.

Management: Okay. They are trying to make an elegant club and are halfway there.

Establishment: This is a grand room that looks like it should be part of Caesars Palace. A large, elegant staircase leads up to the top level, where the VIP rooms are. But the dancers are afraid to walk up or down in their high heels, so if you go up, she will show you to an elevator on the right side of the bar.

On the Cusp – Three Runners Up
Once you wear out your welcome at the Lucky 7, here are three others worth checking out.

8. Cheetah's: Think College Frat Party
Nestled away in an industrial district, Cheetah's is famous as the shoot location for the movie *Showgirls*. This smaller venue is known for their lap dances and party atmosphere.

Dancers: During prime time, it ranges from good to excellent. During daylight hours, it is a bit scary.

Dances: Excellent. Generally, these girls really know how to work it. The clientele is not upscale and they demand a good dance for their hard earned dollar.

<u>Number of Dancers:</u> Cheetah's maintains a solid core of dancers, more than enough to have choices.

<u>Atmosphere:</u> The place is small and loud, so it feels like you are at a party. But because of its size, it is tough to maneuver around during the peak weekend times. Try to get there before 11p.m., because you won't be able to sit down after that. The place is a little grimy, and the clientele is about the same. You will notice a difference when you go here after one of the upscale clubs.

<u>Management:</u> They are cool — they just don't want any problems. Expect to always pay a cover charge here.

<u>Establishment:</u> Very small, and hard to find a place to sit during peak hours. It could use a deep cleaning, because it is an older club and has seen some hard service over many years' use.

9. Olympic Gardens: History in the Making

Located on the Strip just north of the Stratosphere, Olympic Gardens is the mother of all gentlemen's clubs in Vegas. Given its proximity, you may be tempted to walk here if you are on the north part of the Strip. One word: don't. The surrounding area is poorly lit and pretty rough. The club has an upstairs that is for women, where men dancers give their own version of a lap dance.

<u>Dancers:</u> A bit rough around the edges, many of these dancers seem to have graduated from the high-class clubs and moved here. At the other end of the spectrum, you may find a number of green newcomers.

<u>Dances:</u> If you can find a place to get a lap dance, the girls here will give a solid performance. Since lap dance areas are scarce, the dances get a low ranking. You might end up get-

ting a dance on a glorified version of a banquet chair. Not the most comfortable compared with a nice comfy chair at one of the newer places.

Number of Dancers: This place always has a big supply of dancers. There are so many you find them standing around looking for an available body in a seat, of which there are not many. They also congregate at the bar, which can complicate things if you just want to sit, sip a beer and watch the TV. On the other hand, you could be a gentleman and spring for a round of shots.

Atmosphere: Too crowded on weekends for its own good. The crowd here is a bit on the rough side; you might feel like a fight will break out sooner or later. The best part is that women tourists get nutty upstairs with the male dancers and when they leave, they are all wound up and looking to party.

Management: Entry fee is nonnegotiable, even if you drove here. You will receive drink tickets for your entry fee, so be sure to use them up.

Establishment: This place has seen better days. It is falling apart. There is no main stage but a group of smaller circular stages each with chairs surrounding them. Every seat gets taken quickly, and you will find yourself walking around, fighting your way up to the crowded bar to get a drink. The best place to go is the annex room to the immediate left of the entrance. This part of the club is more intimate and has more seats than the main room.

10. Glitter Gulch: Location, Location, Location.
Located right next to Mermaids, in downtown Las Vegas, Glitter Gulch has immediate access. Not the best club in dancers or establishment, but the ability to grab a lap dance while your friends are playing craps makes the Glitter Gulch worth mentioning.

<u>Dancers:</u> Rough, but what can you expect from a club in the middle of downtown Vegas?

<u>Dances:</u> If you can find an average-looking dancer, then you will be set. Otherwise, you will be stuck with a less than desirable. This is a place where you sit back and watch the stage rather than get a dance.

<u>Number of Dancers:</u> This place is small, so there are never that many dancers working. You have to be patient and spot a good dancer who is giving a lap dance, and grab her before somebody else does.

<u>Atmosphere:</u> Not the typical Vegas club. It's more like something you would find in New Orleans. The clientele here is rough, too.

<u>Management:</u> There is a small entry fee of $5 or $10 dollars, but there is a two-drink minimum that you must purchase immediately. They won't help you find a table, so you will be on your own once you walk through the doors.

<u>Establishment:</u> Very small and dark. When you walk in, head right and proceed to the back of the club and find a set of chairs along the wall.

🍸 Classic Vegas Mistake

The Blind Walk: Clubs are very dark inside. If you are entering from the bright sunlight, it will take a while for your eyes to adjust. There is nothing more embarrassing than entering only to walk straight into a wall or table because you can't see. Before you enter, stand outside the doors and close your eyes for about ten seconds. Your eyes will adjust to the darkness, and you will be able to see your way upon entering.

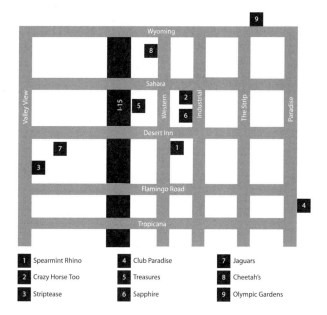

1 Spearmint Rhino	**4** Club Paradise	**7** Jaguars
2 Crazy Horse Too	**5** Treasures	**8** Cheetah's
3 Striptease	**6** Sapphire	**9** Olympic Gardens

Getting There

There are five ways to get to a gentlemen's club. Each one has it benefits and drawbacks.

Walking. There are only a couple of clubs within walking distance of recommended properties: Striptease, if you stay at the Rio; Club Paradise, if you stay at the Hard Rock; and Glitter Gulch, if you are downtown. Sure, you can walk wherever you want, but these are the only three clubs that we recommend walking to.

Taxi. Dropping guys off at gentlemen's clubs is the core of the Vegas taxi business. You are guaranteed to have to pay a cover charge because the taxi drivers get a kickback on all men they bring to clubs.

Chartered Limo. If you charter a limo for the night, you can often get by without paying a cover charge. The money that a group of eight can save will easily pay for the limo for a couple of hours. A limo that is acting as a taxi making one run for you will be treated just like a taxi and you will have to pay cover.

Rental Car. Having a car can save a lot of trouble. It will allow you to go when you want and leave without any trouble. The only drawback is the same you'd encounter anywhere, namely, if no one's willing to be the designated driver, be prepared to leave your rental in the strip club lot and take a cab back to the hotel. Hey, there's no shame in avoiding a DUI and waking up in the Vegas drunk tank.

Club Limo. Some clubs have a limo service that will come pick you up for free and take you to the club. This is a nice way to spruce up your arrival, but you will definitely have to pay the cover.

🍸 Classic Vegas Mistake

Taxi Driver's Advice on Which Club to Choose: Never go where the taxi driver wants you to go. The information in this book is all the advice that you need. The taxi driver's advice is flawed because each club gives the driver a kickback for bringing men there. Most of the kickbacks are $20, but some of the worst clubs can even kick back up to $50.

When to Go

The Gentlemen's club world is made up of four 6-hour shifts. During each shift the club has a distinctly different energy and vibe created by the number, quality and energy of the girls.

<u>Prime Time: 9 p.m.–3 a.m.</u> These are the witching hours when you will have the largest number of the hottest, most alluring girls vying for your attention and your dollars. It is also the time that the club will be packed and it will be difficult to get a seat.

<u>Graveyard: 3 a.m.–9 a.m.</u> There are some diamonds in the rough here, but overall, the level of dancer drops significantly from prime time. Occasionally, some prime timers stay over a couple more hours to earn some extra money. Although, just like casinos, a strip club has no windows and no clocks to break the spell, as 3 a.m. imperceptibly, inevitably, turns to 7 a.m., you will definitely get the feeling you're trapped in a bad vampire movie.

<u>Midday: 9 a.m.–3 p.m.</u> The worst of the four shifts. Every club is empty, the girls are pathetic and the vacuum of a cleaning crew will be in your way. Few clubs have anything good going during these hours.

<u>Happy Hour: 3 p.m.–9 p.m.</u> The second-best shift, especially on weekends. A good number of pretty girls. The last hours of the Happy Hour are the best as some of the prime timers come in early.

🍸 Classic Vegas Mistake

Tipping $5s and $20s onstage: Onstage with all the flashing lights, a girl can't see what bill you are giving her, and once she does realize that someone gave her a $20, she won't know where she got it in the first place. Dancers in Vegas are glad to get any money when they are onstage, so stick with the $1s.

The $20 Lap Dance

The lap dance in Las Vegas is a dance where the stripper is giving you a personalized dance. It lasts the duration of one song. She will start by taking her clothes off in front off you, except for her panties. Then she will perform a series of moves with her body: some moves will involve contact with your body, others will not. At the end of the song, the stripper puts her clothes back on. You then to proceed to pay her $20.

$20 for one song? Does $20 sound expensive to you? When in Vegas, it is one of the best deals around.

Taking a Break

Some of the girls can be very aggressive in their pursuit of your dollars. Perhaps you're looking for a break, a chance to take it all in, and you want to be left alone. There are a couple of things you can do to get the girls to pass you up as a sales lead.

1. Cross Your Legs

The standard approach is for the girls to come over and have a seat on your lap as they make their pitch. Although some ladies are bold enough to sit on your lap anyway, many will take your posture as a sign to move on.

2. Light Up a Cigar

A cigar can serve as your lifeboat. Puffing on a big stogie, emitting gratuitous amounts of secondhand smoke, is a great way to get people to leave you alone.

3. Engage in a "Business" Conversation

If you and your buddies are involved in a deep conversation about stock derivatives, then the dancer will usually leave you alone until you stop talking. Use this to your advantage when you see some less than desirables coming your way.

Don't Act Like a Jerk

Just like every other place in Las Vegas, a lot of guys feel like they can do just about anything inside a gentlemen's club. Well, you can do whatever you want, just as long as you don't like your nose very much. Look, everyone likes to cut loose and whoop it up inside — this is perfectly acceptable. Just remember, you better not get too out of line. Taking it too far could cause you bodily harm, as the bouncers don't have a very good sense of humor. Only touch a dancer on the legs, arms, and waist: Everything else can be construed as too aggressive.

☟ Classic Vegas Mistake

Not having $20 bills: You need to be able to pay for your dance right then and there. Don't give the dancer a $50 or a $100 bill and ask for change. She might think that the extra money is a tip and refuse to give the change back to you. This is an old trick that dancers play on drunken men. While that's worst-case, at best you're going to have to wait around while she goes to get change, and she will not be in a hurry.

Comparing Lap Dances to Gambling

When you are in Vegas, you are going to gamble. You can gamble away $20 at a gaming table in a matter of seconds. So, would you rather spend a couple of minutes at a blackjack table or a couple of minutes having a hot chick all over you? You can take the $100 that you blow at a blackjack table in a half hour and turn that into an entire night of incredible memories at a gentlemen's club.

> ### ☐ Classic Vega Mistake
>
> **Getting a dance when the song is half over:** When you ask girls for a dance, make sure she starts on the next song, not the current song. Many a sucker's gotten a one-minute lap dance and had to pay full price. Use the time before they start dancing to your advantage and strike up a conversation with them.

Buying Drinks for Dancers

If the dancer is sincerely going to sit and talk to you, it is okay to buy her a drink. Some dancers will ask for a drink once you've denied them a lap dance, just so they don't have to buy it themselves. Don't give her a drink if you think she's just going to walk away with it.

> ### ☐ Classic Vegas Mistake
>
> **The Two-Girl Dance:** The two-girl dance sounds like a fantasy, right? A once-in-a-lifetime, letter to Penthouse kind of event that will leave you spent, dumbstruck, and happy. In actuality, the two-girl dance is a waste of money, because it reduces the amount of physical interaction you will get. If you think about it, there's really only room for one on your lap, so each girl will be trying to each do her own thing and you'll be wondering why you're wasting your money. You'll wind up paying for two bad dancers instead of one good one. Pass on this one.

☎ BEYOND THE GENTLEMEN'S CLUBS

Gentlemen's clubs aren't the only place in Vegas where you can pay for the privilege of beautiful, naked girls dancing all over you. There are other, more daring options.

Dancers to Your Room

A staple of many bachelor parties is having a dancer come to your hotel room to perform a dance routine and cheesy games with the bachelor.

Getting a Dancer to Your Room

Calling a Service. The Vegas yellow pages are filled with "Dancers Direct to You" ads. Be sure to talk about rates and the type of girl that you want. Charges are incurred, and the clock starts ticking once she's in the room. If they send someone you are less than satisfied with, then don't let her through the door.

The Casino Bar. From about 11 at night until 4 in the morning, all the working girls congregate at the center bar in each casino. You will be able to spot them because they will be sitting by themselves drinking a non-alcoholic beverage such as hot tea or cappuccino. Approach them with negotiation in mind, since these girls are here to work and don't want to sit and talk to you. The later the hour of the night (or morning), the more the price will come down.

Brothels

It is a lingering misconception that prostitution is legal in Las Vegas. It isn't. In most of the state of Nevada, it is legal; however, in Clark County, where Vegas resides, it is not. Brothels are legalized venues where you may purchase the services of a prostitute, located on the outskirts of Las Vegas, just over the county line. It takes about an hour to get to any brothel from the Strip.

The Brothel Experience

The "Grand" Entrance. When you enter, the madam will make an announcement of your arrival to all the girls not currently working in the private rooms. The girls will stop their conversations and line up in front of you. The madam will proceed to announce the name of each girl to you. At this point, you may choose a girl you like, but don't feel pressured if you don't see the right one. Just say thank you and proceed to the bar for a drink.

The Lounge Area. This is the congregating area for the girls and clients. Here, the girls will engage you and get to know you. After a while, they will ask if you want a tour of the property or want to go someplace more intimate. If you are going to proceed to buy a service, negotiate out in the lounge area before you proceed to the private rooms. Use the buddy system here to bail out your friends if it's apparent they're getting into something they don't want to do.

The Private Rooms. These are the rooms where the girls do their entertaining. Some are quite lavish rooms decked out with a variety of décor, such as an "Egyptian room," or "Jungle Room." In these rooms you will be asked up front for payment for services before you start.

Brothel Tips

Don't be pressured. This is a legal transaction, regulated by the state of Nevada. As the customer, you are in the driver's seat here because you hold the cash. Don't do something with someone that you really don't want to. If you've just come from a strip club in town, you will notice right away that there's a big comedown in the quality of the girls out here in the sticks. If that looks good to you, go for it. If not, have a drink in the lounge and be on your way.

Negotiate. Everything is negotiable. Pretend she is a car salesman and never take her first offer. Ask for add-ins like a bottle of champagne, a lap dance, or thirty minutes in the hot tub. There is more to do other than just having sex.

<u>Take our advice, and avoid:</u> Look, if your idea of fun is driving an hour or so each way to pay for sex with a less-than-attractive woman, I guess we can't stop you. But we'd sure like to try. The brothel scene is pathetic; what you have, at base, is a bunch of strip club rejects in a glorified double-wide trailer in the desert. Save what little dignity you have left, and pass.

🍸 Classic Vegas Mistake

The Brothel Crawl: If you're unsatisfied with the quality of the girls at the brothel (you will be), don't leave and go to the next one in search of something better. All you'll find is another group of girls identical to the ones you just left. There is no "better." Face it: If a girl were really hot she'd be making a lot more money dancing in the clubs. Seeking nirvana in a brothel is a lost cause.

PART III

Viva Las Vegas

Chapter 10

Running on Empty

✶ ....

By the end of your trip you'll realize the only thing worse than not spending enough time in Las Vegas is spending too much time in Las Vegas. Once you've given it all you have (and hopefully have left without spending your entire life savings), its time to head home. If you plan ahead, you'll leave here wanting to come back; if you don't, the end of your trip could be so miserable that...who are we kidding? You're going to want to come back. But figuring out when to leave is important.

> ### 🍸 Classic Vegas Mistake
>
> **Leaving Too Far Apart:** Most groups make their travel reservations separately, and only realize when it's time to leave that they're leaving twelve hours apart. Huge mistake. At this point either your group is busted up, leaving you to spend a few hours of idle time in the airport or sit around in your hotel lobby because you've been kicked out of your room. Make sure everyone is leaving at approximately the same time.

You'll Need More Rest

You've stayed out later and gotten by on less sleep than you have in years. Good job: You've soaked as much life out of this town as you can. The flip side of your adventure is that it'll catch up with you fast. If at all possible, try to get a half-day or day off to serve as a buffer on your return. Otherwise you'll roll into the office looking like Nick Nolte's DUI mug shot and will feel like work is even more horrific than usual. There's a good chance that the annoying office dullard who swings by your desk a half-dozen times a day will go home in a neck brace when you lose it on him as he inquires endlessly about your trip. Avoid the workplace violence that could cost you your job, and get some time to readjust to civilization before your return to work.

Checking Out of Your Hotel

- ✤ When you check out, don't waste your time standing in the long line at the front desk. Use the check out on your television or just leave and have the bill put on your credit card.

- ✤ Check-out times are not set in stone. If they say check-out time is 10 a.m., don't worry if is it 11 a.m. before you roll out. If they call your room just tell them that you are packing up your stuff.

- ✤ If your flight leaves later, check your bags in with the bellboy. If you are going to spend the rest of your time at a different hotel before you leave, bring your bags with you and check them in with the bell desk at that hotel. You don't have to be a guest there to check your bags.

Stay-Over Rates

If you're leaving on Sunday, most hotels offer really cheap stay-over rates. Can you extend your stay an extra day and leave on Monday? Changing your ticket might not be too expensive. Leave on Monday morning when the lines are shorter, or consider keeping the room but not staying overnight. If your departure time is late at night, maybe it's worth paying for an extra night to keep your room until you have to leave for the airport.

The alternative is checking out of your room, checking your bags at the front desk, and wandering around. If your friends have to leave earlier, don't head over to the airport with them just to face the tightest slots in town for a few hours. Keep the room, sleep in, hang out, watch some *Sports Center*, hit the pool, take a nap, take a shower, check out, and head for the airport. If you're leaving late but weren't able to finagle a day's worth of breathing room between your return home and your return to work, at least you can rest up a bit.

It's not fun to check out and check your bags. You can't go to the pool anymore, and if you do you won't be able to shower before your flight. You're probably getting tired of your hotel, but you can't stray too far because you'll have to come back for your bags, or even worse, have to lug your luggage up and down the Strip. Chances are you'll wind up sitting alone at the sportsbook, looking so disheveled that no one will talk to you.

TIME TO FLY: The Sunday Airport Blues

Leaving Las Vegas on Sunday can be brutal. While the city is amazing in its ability to draw people in, chew them up, and spit them back out as it prepares for new arrivals with great efficiency, that efficiency doesn't extend to airport departures. Though McCarran is a well-run airport, the Sunday crowds are overwhelming.

Not only is there a ton of people leaving, everyone is broke, tired, hung over, and hungry. A lot of people have not slept, and their B.O. fills the air. You hear people coughing everywhere because everyone smokes in Vegas, even people who usually never smoke. Their bodies are going through rejection. On top of the secondhand smoke inhalation, the lack of sleep, and the disheveled appearance, everyone is downright pissed. The excitement and energy that filled the air on your arrival is gone. Replacing it is a morbid environment of grumpy people who just want to get home. You don't want to spend one second more than you have to in McCarran on Sunday.

🍸 Classic Vegas Mistake

Checking Luggage: Remember this mistake from earlier in the book? If you didn't heed the warning the first time, you spent some time at the baggage terminal when you arrived. Well, that was just the tip of the iceberg. Checking your bags on your flight home can be brutal. The lines are long, so arrive early. Hopefully your need to check luggage isn't the result of your deciding to take home a bunch of yard-long margarita glasses, because that'd be just plain pathetic.

If you absolutely have to leave on a Sunday, here are a few tips to make it a bit more bearable:

1. Leave Early
Getting in and out of the airport early can help you avoid the masses. If you can get a flight out before 9 a.m., take it.

2. Leave Late
Aside from early morning, late night is the second calmest time of the day. Anytime after 7 p.m. is the way to go.

3. Don't Plan to Eat at the Airport
Most guys plan to get that last bite to eat at the airport before they leave. Don't do it. The lines are long and full of angry, hung over people just like you.

Computer Check-In

McCarran International Airport offers that latest in check-in technology. All you need is your credit card and flight information. At every entrance to the building are computer terminals that will print you a boarding pass to every single airline. Use this to avoid the check-in lines and get your boarding pass fast. The one caveat is that you can only have carry-on luggage: another good reason not to check your bags.

Airport Loitering

Whatever you do, don't head over to the airport with your friends if their flights depart hours before yours. This is a popular, miserable mistake. You'll be stuck in an overcrowded airport just trying to kill time. The upside of not checking your bags was avoiding a couple of long lines; the downside of not checking your bags is that you're stuck dragging them around. You'll have to drag your bags with you as you amble from the newsstand, to the bar, to the fast-food counter, and back to the newsstand in your attempt to kill time. At this point you'll probably have managed to burn off forty minutes of the five-hour wait for your plane to board.

Avoid the misery and let your friends go on without you. You're a big boy, you can find your way to the airport. Of course, if you'd have booked yourself on the right flight, you wouldn't be stuck in this situation, but hey you don't need anyone to belabor that glaring oversight.

Driving out of Town

The key to driving home is the same as flying: Leave early and avoid Sunday traveling. If you're heading back to L.A. the drive can be hectic. Everyone is in a rush to get nowhere, and everyone is hung over and sleep-deprived, so drive very carefully. One accident can set you back hours. If at all possible, avoid driving out of Las Vegas on Sundays.

🍸 Classic Vegas Mistake

Taking the Oversold Flight Offer: Flights out of Vegas are often oversold. The gate attendant will be offering a free travel voucher, a free hotel room, and a flight out the next day. Unless you've already negotiated the day off on Monday, don't be seduced by this offer. You will be tempted to push on with your Vegas experience with one last hurrah at the gaming tables. But remember: You are by yourself, out of money, and bone-tired. Your body is torn up and ready to go home. Your extended vacation won't be worth remembering. On the other hand, if you've got the free time and want to use it to recuperate, so be it.

O_2 Recharge

There's an Oxygen Bar located in the C Terminal at McCarran. We can't vouch for its effects, but they claim that the O_2 boost will help clean out your polluted mind. Just a thought if you have a few extra minutes and ten bucks to kill. Who knows, this might be just what you need if you're returning home to a dinner with the in-laws or a job interview.

SOAK IT UP THREE WAYS ON SUNDAY

If you are leaving late on Sunday, here are a few options to spend your time.

Option 1: Strip Clubs

Nothing beats spending your last hours in a dark strip club with good music, sports on the Tvs, and hot strippers. Strip clubs of choice for Sundays are Crazy Horse Too and Striptease. On Sundays, both offer a relaxed environment with discounted drink prices, lots of TVs with sports, and laid-back strippers who won't pressure you into a dance.

Option 2: Gambling

If you have a couple of hours you're looking to burn, gambling on Sundays is a great option. The table minimums go back down to $5. Play a slow game like pai gow poker and try to grind out a couple bucks. The best places to play on Sunday are Hard Rock, given its close proximity to the airport, and New York-New York, because it provides a low-key environment.

Option 3: Massage

Schedule a massage for after you check out, and spend a couple of hours detoxifying. Take your time in the steam room, soak in the hot tub, and get a massage. Eat the complimentary fresh fruit and drink as much water as possible. Not only will your body be recuperating, you will also be able to take a nice long hot shower and change your clothes just before you leave for the airport.

Chapter 11

Tales to Tell

✳ ....

Okay, so you finally made it back to work. You're in your cube, you're hung over, you didn't make enough money playing black-jack to retire (although it certainly seemed like a distinct possibility at 4 o'clock on Sunday morning), so now you have to face the world again. Assume two things: 1) You'll get nothing productive done on Monday morning; 2) You'd better have something to tell the guys at lunch.

Stories Are Expected and Anticipated

You can't come home without a few good tales to tell. If you followed anything at all in the preceding pages, you will have a few whoppers to lay on the guys from accounting. Without you even knowing it, they sat around on Saturday morning, as their wives forced them to clean out the garage, and cursed your name. Your whereabouts were on the minds of every guy and gal you know back at home who had even an inkling of your plans to hit Sin City. So, as you return to civilization, a poorer, wiser, partied-out man with a Texas-size grin on your face, you owe them some dirt. If you come home without something to say, these sad, pathetic, vicarious sacks will probably wish you just didn't bother to come home at all. They are dying to hear what you have to say, so don't disappoint them.

 ## YOUR DUTY

Once you've been back for a couple of days, you'll probably tell
the story about Jimmy trying to hook up with one of the chicks
from the *Sirens of TI* show about two dozen times. Not that it's
not a great story — I mean, come on, it's not every day that you
get shot down by a pirate. Once that initial euphoria has worn
off, it's time to own up to your responsibilities.

Come Clean

Why do so many people spend half a day in line trying to get to
the top of Stratosphere? Why do so many guys go to Rain, only
to spend a whole night waiting in an unending line? Because
someone, somewhere told them it was a good idea. Just because
you got suckered doesn't mean that you should let a friend, ac-
quaintance, or perfect stranger suffer the same fate. If something
sucked, admit it.

Don't spread Vegas Hype. What is Vegas Hype? Vegas Hype is a
certain type of B.S.: it's like P.T. Barnum on steroids, an other-
worldly level of mistruth that puts lies about any other town to
shame. Las Vegas is built on guys and gals coming back and
telling someone that they had "the time of their life" or "the best

meal at" a place that sucked, because they won't admit that they were conned. Just like any get-rich-quick or rapid-weight-loss scam, most people are embarrassed to admit that they were taken advantage of. Be a man: admit it, when pressed, that something was a rip-off or a complete waste of time.

♟ Classic Vegas Mistake

Bringing Back What Happened in Vegas: One of the biggest disservices you can do to your fellow Vegas veterans is airing their dirty laundry. There exists a code among men, and within that code is a clause that clearly states: "A Man cannot share embarrassing details about his fellow Man without that Man being present." It goes on to state that you cannot share salacious (and true) tidbits with spouses or girlfriends. Trust us, your buddy didn't decide to do some crazy stuff out of sight of his wife's watchful eyes with the intention of going home and telling her about it. It's a known fact that the three biggest causes for divorce are money, infidelity, and Vegas. Do everyone a favor and adhere to the maxim "What happens in Vegas . . ." — you know the rest. Those commercials aren't part of a marketing campaign, they're public service announcements.

Spread the Truth

Okay, you've finally admitted it: You overpaid for dinner on Saturday night. One of the knuckleheads convinced you to veer off our path, and you paid dearly. Not only is it something you have to admit to yourself and others, it's something that you need to spread the truth about. Don't confess your dark secrets; share them with everyone you know. Whenever you hear the words "Las Vegas" you owe it to others to say "We had a great time following the advice of the *Las Vegas Little Black Book*: but we did go against their advice once and got burned." You have to tell others. Some of the lamest things in Vegas thrive solely because no one is willing to admit the truth, so fess up.

HOW TO TELL A VEGAS STORY

Vegas stories tend to be unique. Guys let loose in a big way, resulting in wild tales. If you tell it well, a Vegas story will play much better than your daily, idle, reality-show recap, water cooler chit chat.

Think About The Little Things

While the action is big and often dramatic, as with any good story, the success of a Vegas yarn lies in the details. Did an Elvis impersonator cut in front of you at the buffet? Did you order a bottle of champagne for a group of girls just before their boyfriends joined them at their table? Did one of you almost get married at a chapel? (This never happens, by the way.) Were you able to score big with a limo and roll around the Strip like high rollers? Did you make a crazy gambling wager that paid for your trip or broke you? (Probably not.) Did you eat an unusual Vegas item like a chocolate-covered, deep-fried Twinkie? The more unusual the better when it comes to Vegas.

Start from the Beginning

The story begins at the airport, on the plane, and getting to your hotel. You need a casual buildup before you knock them out with a big punch.

Hit the Key Points

If you followed the advice of this book, then your trip was action-packed with many different events. When you tell the story, people won't believe that you were able to do so many things in such a short amount of time. You planned properly, though, and you eliminated the wasted time wandering, sitting in taxis and waiting around that all the other Vegas visitors did.

Finish with a Bang

The end of your story should end with a highlight of your trip —
not with you sitting in the airport for a couple of hours trying to
get back. Other people are going to want to come to Vegas with
you once you tell them your tales.

1 PLAN YOUR NEXT TRIP

Now that you have experienced Vegas *Black Book* style, it's time
to take some time to insure you next trip will be even better.

Put it in Writing

Take notes, something that you can pass along to your buddies.
Take time in the days after your return to jot down what you
liked and what you didn't. As you know, there are way too many
options in this town. Your detailed descriptions could save
someone you know time and money.

Help Us Help You

If you were suckered in by the Strip, conned at a cabaret show,
or taken in by a topless bar, we need to know. Log on to **www.ve-
gaslittleblackbook.com** and tell us your story. We'll get the
word out and make sure others benefit from your mistake. If you
had a great time (of course you did, if you followed our advice)
we want to know about that, too. Sign up for our newsletter. We
promise to keep you up to date on all of the hits and misses in
Sin City.

RETURN!

Give yourself a few days to recover, and then start planning your
next trip to Las Vegas. Trust us, now that you know how to do
Vegas right, the next trip will be even better.

Itineraries:
Follow the Plan

✴ ....

 LITTLE BLACK BOOK ITINERARIES

With so many choices in Vegas, it is difficult to make a plan for the entire trip. These six itineraries are designed for you to follow or use as your base for your Vegas weekend.

Medium Rollers

The medium roller is a person who wants to focus on gambling for his trip, not just drop a couple of quarters in a slot machine or two.

<u>Accommodations:</u> Treasure Island

<u>Group Size:</u> 3–5

Day 1: Practice Makes Perfect

    8:00 p.m. — Arrival into Vegas

    9:00 p.m. — Check into hotel

    9:30 p.m. — Fuel up at the snack shop

  10:00 p.m. — Play some low stakes craps

  12:00 a.m. — Drinks at the center bar

    1:00 a.m. — Play pai gow poker with your group until the place clears out

    2:00 a.m. — Play $5 blackjack to get your mind in gear for the next day

    3:00 a.m. — Sleep

Day 2: Make your Move

10:00 a.m. — Meal at the coffee Shop
11:00 a.m. — Play $25 double deck blackjack
1:00 p.m. — Hit the sportsbook and make some bets on the early east coast games.
2:00 p.m. — Play $25 pai gow poker
3:00 p.m. — Early lunch at the buffet
4:00 p.m. — Play in low stakes poker tournament
5:00 p.m. — Cash in sports bets, make bets on the west coast games
6:00 p.m. — Shower and change clothes. Meet up at the Center bar, rested up for the big run.
7:00 p.m. — Play $50 blackjack
9:00 p.m. — Play $10 craps
10:00 p.m. — Play $100 blackjack
11:00 p.m. — Cash in on sports bets, hit snack bar for quick bite
11:30 p.m. — Play $100 blackjack
1:00 a.m. — Center bar for a drink to cool down
2:00 a.m. — Play $10 Craps
3:00 a.m. — Late night meal in the coffee shop
4:00 a.m. — Sleep

Day 3: Double It Up

10:00 a.m. — Have room service bring coffee to room
11:00 a.m. — Check out
12:00 p.m. — Eat lunch at the ethic restaurant
1:00 p.m. — Play $10 single deck blackjack
3:00 p.m. — Chase your losses or press your wins with a huge departure bet on roulette
4:00 p.m. — Airport and depart

Adrenaline Junkies

The adrenaline junkie wants a rush. Be it gambling, women or thrill rides, this guy wants to feel his heart pumping with fast-paced action and high stakes.

Accommodations: New York–New York
Group Size: 4–8

Day 1: Start off with a Bang
    6:00 p.m. — Arrival into Vegas
    7:00 p.m. — Check into hotel
    7:30 p.m. — A substantial arrival bet on roulette
    8:00 p.m. — Big bet on two games in the sportsbook
    8:30 p.m. — New York-New York roller coaster
    9:00 p.m. — Dinner at the ethnic restaurant where you can watch the games
    11:00 a.m. — Hit the dueling piano bar to try to pick up some girls
    2:00 a.m. — Play craps
    3:00 a.m. — Sleep

Day 2: Make your Move
    10:00 a.m. — Wake up
    11:00 a.m. — Take on the buffet in an all you eat contest
    1:00 p.m. — Watch an extreme sports movie at the Imax Theatre at Luxor.
    2:00 p.m. — Taxi to Stratosphere
    2:00 p.m. — Ride all four rides in this order: High Roller roller coaster, X Scream, Insanity and Big Shot.
    4:00 p.m. — Play blackjack at the Sahara
    5:00 p.m. — Ride SPEED The Ride at Sahara
    6:00 p.m. — Shower and change clothes. Meet up at the center bar for drinks.
    8:00 p.m. — Blue Man Group
    10:00 p.m. — Dinner at the steak house
    12:00 p.m. — Irish pub for drinks and women
    1:00 p.m. — Big Apple Bar to dance with drunk women
    3:00 a.m. — Sleep

Day 3: Guns and a Massage

    10:00 a.m. — Room service to the room

    11:00 a.m. — Check out; give bags to the bellman

    12:00 p.m. — Taxi to the Gun Store for some machine-gun shooting

    2:00 p.m. — Massage, steam, and sauna at the spa

    5:00 p.m. — Airport and departure

Rat Packers

The Rat Packers want to relive old-school Vegas. The days of Frankie, Dean, and Sammy can still be found in Vegas. Ring-a-ding-ding.

<u>Accommodations:</u> Caesars Palace

<u>Group Size:</u> 3–6

Day 1: Roll in style

    8:00 p.m. — Arrival into Vegas

    9:00 p.m. — Limo ride to Caesars, check into big suite

    10:00 p.m. — Fontana Lounge at Bellagio for appetizers, cigars and martinis

    3:00 a.m. — Sleep

Day 2: Go All Class

    1:00 p.m. — Hit the spa for a steam

    2:00 p.m. — Late lunch at the pool cafe

    4:00 p.m. — Shop for a new outfit

    5:00 p.m. — Shave at the Art of Shaving

    6:00 p.m. — Shoe shine

    6:30 p.m. — Limo to Del Frisco's

    7:00 p.m. — Pre-dinner Martini

    7:30 p.m. — Steak dinner

    9:00 p.m. — Cigars and an after-dinner drink

    10:00 p.m. — Late show with Wayne Newton

    12:00 a.m. — Craps

    2:00 a.m. — Sleep

Day 3: Soak it Up

    10:00 a.m. — Have room service bring coffee to room

    12:00 p.m. — Check out

1:00 p.m. — Pool side for sun and Bloody Marys.

4:00 p.m. — Airport and departure

Champagne Taste on a Beer Budget

For those who want to live the high life but not have pay for it.

<u>Accommodations:</u> Rio

<u>Group Size:</u> 4–12

Day 1:

6:00 p.m. — Arrival into Vegas

7:00 p.m. — Check in to Rio

8:00 p.m. — Appetizers and drinks at an ethnic restaurant

10:00 p.m. — Drinks at the center bar

12:00 p.m. — Voodoo Lounge

3:00 a.m. — Sleep

Day 2: Limo It Up

11:00 a.m. — Poolside for Bloody Marys and lunch

1:00 p.m. — Blackjack

3:00 p.m. — Change clothes

4:00 p.m. — Cocktails at the center bar

5:00 p.m. — Craps

7:00 p.m. — Charter limo for the night

8:00 p.m. — Headline comedian

10:00 p.m. — Steak dinner at Hugo's Cellar

12:00 a.m. — Striptease gentleman's Club

4:00 a.m. — Sleep

Day 3:

10:00 a.m. — Breakfast at the coffee shop

12:00 p.m. — Check out

1:00 p.m. — Poolside for sun and relaxation

3:00 p.m. — Spa for sauna and shower

4:00 p.m. — Airport and departure

Sports Fanatics

Sports fanatics live and breathe sports. Since Las Vegas is the only place in the country where sports wagering is legal, this itinerary is focused around the sportsbook.

<u>Accommodations:</u> Mandalay Bay

<u>Group Size:</u> 4–12

Day 1:

    5:00 p.m. — Arrival into Vegas

    6:00 p.m. — Check into Mandalay Bay

    7:00 p.m. — Sportsbook for wagers on the games

  10:00 p.m. — Blackjack

  12:00 p.m. — Cocktail at center bar

    3:00 a.m. — Sleep

Day 2: The Big Event

  10:00 a.m. — Wake up and watch Sportcenter

  11:00 a.m. — Sportsbook for afternoon games

  12:00 p.m. — Lunch at ESPN Zone

    3:00 p.m. — Bet the afternoon games in the Sportsbook

    5:00 p.m. — Cocktails at the center bar

    6:00 p.m. — Steak dinner in the Foundation Room

    8:00 p.m. — Boxing Match at Manadalay Bay Events
                       Center

  11:00 p.m. — House of Blues

    1:00 a.m. — Craps

    2:00 a.m. — Sleep

Day 3: Bet the Ponies

    9:00 a.m. — Have room service bring coffee to room

  10:00 a.m. — Sportsbook for horse betting

  12:00 p.m. — Check out

    1:00 p.m. — Sportbook for more horse betting

    2:00 p.m. — Lunch at the snack shop

    4:00 p.m. — Airport and departure

Night Crawlers

Night Crawlers want to take in as much of the Vegas nightlife as possible.

Accommodations: Hard Rock
Group Size: 3–6

Day 1: Start Drinking
    5:00 p.m. — Arrival into Vegas
    6:00 p.m. — Check into Hard Rock
    7:00 p.m. — Drinks at the center bar
    8:00 p.m. — Dinner at Pink Taco
  10:00 p.m. — Drinks at the center bar
  11:00 p.m. — Buy a Table at Body English nightclub
    3:00 a.m. — Club Paradise gentleman's club
    5:00 a.m. — Late-night meal at Mr. Lucky's
    6:00 a.m. — Sleep

Day 2: Keep Drinking
    4:00 p.m. — Wake up
    6:00 p.m. — Dinner at Simon Kitchen
    8:00 p.m. — Craps
    9:00 p.m. — Drinks at the center bar
  10:00 p.m. — Limo to Strip, party in the limo
  11:00 p.m. — Carnival Court at Harrah's
    1:00 a.m. — Spearmint Rhino
    3:00 a.m. — Drinks and appetizers at Peppermill Fireside
                      Lounge
    5:00 a.m. — Blackjack
    6:00 a.m. — Sleep

Day 3: Catch the Late Flight
  12:00 a.m. — Have room service bring breakfast to room
    2:00 p.m. — Hit pool for margaritas
    4:00 p.m. — Late check out
    5:00 p.m. — Dinner at coffee shop
    6:00 p.m. — Blackjack
    7:00 p.m. — Crazy Horse Too
  10:00 p.m. — Airport and departure

Little Black Book Lists: Your Reference Guide

✶ ....

These lists are based on the top places for groups of guys. Other places in Vegas may be just as good — or even better — for other purposes, but are omitted here because they don't fit the special needs of men. Use these lists as your reference when arranging plans and making reservations.

Best Accommodations

Mandalay Bay	877-632-7800
	www.mandalaybay.com
TI	800-288-7206
	www.treasureisland.com
Caesars	800-634-6661
	www.caesars.com
Hard Rock	800-HRD-ROCK
	www.hardrockhotel.com
MGM Grand	877-880-0880
	www.mgmgrand.com
Rio	800-PLAY-RIO
	www.riolasvegas.com
New York–New York	866-815-4365
	www.nynyhotelcasino.com
Flamingo	888-308-8899
	www.flamingolasvegas.com

Harrah's	800-634-6765
	www.harrahs.com
Monte Carlo	888-529-4828
	www.montecarlo.com

Best Gentlemen's Clubs

Spearmint Rhino	702-796-3600
	www.spearmintrhino.com
Crazy Horse Too	702-382-8003
Striptease	702-253-1555
	www.stripteasevegas.com
Club Paradise	702-734-7990
	www.clubparadise.net
Treasures	702-257-3030
	www.treasureslasvegas.com
Sapphires	702-796-6000
	www.sapphirelasvegas.com
Jaguar's	702-367-4000
	www.jaguarslv.com
Cheetah's	702-384-0074
	www.cheetahsnv.com
Olympic Gardens	702-385-8987
	www.ogvegas.com
Glitter Gulch	702-385-4774

Best Center Bars

Breeze Bar at TI
Seahorse Lounge at Caesars
Kuri at MGM
Parasol Up at Wynn
Centrifuge at MGM
Baccarat Bar at Bellagio

Best Nightclubs/ Bars
Carnival Court at Harrah's
Kaunaville at TI
Voodoo Lounge at Rio
Dueling Piano Bar at NewYork–NewYork
House of Blues at Mandalay
Margaritaville at Flamingo
Dueling piano bar at Harrah's
Coral Lounge at Mandalay
The Beach
Cleopatra's Barge at Caesars Palace

Best Pools
Mandalay Bay
Flamingo
Hard Rock
MGM Grand
Rio
Wynn
Caesars
Mirage

Best 24-hour Coffee Shops
Mr. Lucky's at Hard Rock
The Bellagio Café
Grand Lux at the Venetian
Peppermill   (702) 735-4177
Café Lago at Caesars
Sao Paulo at Rio
Terrace Pointe Café at Wynn
Raffles Café at Mandalay Bay

Best Buffets
Dishes at TI
Cravings at Mirage
The Buffet at Mandalay Bay

Luxor Buffet
Rio Around the World Buffet
Golden Nugget
Bellagio Buffet
The Buffet at Wynn

Best Steak houses

The Steakhouse at Circus Circus	702-794-3767
Hugo's Cellar at Four Queens	702-385-4011
Peiro's	702-369-2305
Smith & Wollenskys	702-862-4100
Capital Grill at Fashion Show Mall	702-932-6631
Lawry's The Prime Rib	702-893-2223
Austin's at Texas Station	702-631-1033
Del Frisco's	702-796-0063
A.J.'s Steakhouse at Hard Rock	702-693-5500
Gallagher's at New York–New York	702-740-6450

Best Ethnic restaurants

Isla at TI (New Age Mexican)
Okada at Wynn (Sushi)
Gonzalez y Gonzalez at New York–New York (Mexican)
Mesa Grill at MGM Grand (Southwest fusion)
Simon Kitchen at Hard Rock (American)
Pink Taco at Hard Rock (Mexican)
Pearl at MGM Grand (Chinese)
808 at Caesars (Hawaiian fusion)

Best Snack Bars

Canter's Delicatessen at TI
Snack shop at Bellagio
Toscano's Grill at Rio
Carnegie at Mirage

Best Places to Have the Big Meal

Smith & Wollenskys	702-862-4100
Capital Grill at Fashion Show Mall	702-932-6631
Foundation Room at Mandalay Bay	702-632-4803
Del Frisco's	702-796-0063
Okada at Wynn	702-770-3320
Austin's at Texas Station	702-631-1033

Best Places for Blackjack

Casino Royal	800-854-7666
	www.casinoroyalehotel.com
New Frontier	800-634-6966
	www.fontierlv.com
Barbary Coast	888-227-2279
	www.barbarycoastcasino.com
Horseshoe	800-937-6537
	www.binons.com
New York–New York	
Hard Rock	

Best Places for Craps

Horseshoe	
Hard Rock	
New York–New York	
Casino Royale	
Golden Nugget	800-634-3403
	www.goldennugget.com
TI	

Best Sportsbooks

MGM Grand	
Mandalay Bay	
Stardust	800-634-6757
	www.stardustlv.com
Hard Rock	
ESPN Zone at New York–New York	
Caesars	

Best Shows

Blue Man Group	800-557-7428
Penn & Teller	888-746-7784
The Amazing Jonathan	702-737-2515
Headline Comedians	
Mystère	702-796-9999
Wayne Newton	888-222-5361
Tournament of Kings	702-597-7600

Best Topless Shows

Le Femme at MGM Grand	800-929-1111
Crazy Girls at Rivera	702-794-9433
Skintight at Harrah's	800-392-9002 ext. 5222
Midnight Fantasy at Luxor	702-262-4400
Bite at Stratosphere	702-380-7777

Best Places to Smoke a Cigar

Del Frisco's Cigar Lounge	702-796-0063
Baccarat Bar at Bellagio	702-693-7111
Mon Ami Gabi's Patio at Paris	702-944-4224
Prime Steakhouse's outdoor patio at Bellagio	702-791-7223
Foundation Room's Balcony at Mandalay Bay	702-632-7777
Austin's A-Bar at Texas Station	702-631-1033
Casa Fuente at Caesars	702-731-5051

Best Nightclubs to Buy a Bottle

Light at Bellagio	702-693-8300
Tabu at MGM Grand	702-891-1111
Vivid at Venetian	702-414-1000
Pure at Caesars	702-731-7110
Foundation Room at Mandalay Bay *(Members Only except Mondays)*	702-632-7777
Tangerine at TI	702-894-7111

Best Places to Shoot Guns

The Gun Store   702-454-1110
            www.thegunstorelasvegas.com
Boulder Rifle & Pistol Club 702-293-1885
            www.brpc1.org

Best Helicopter Companies

Maverick Helicopters   888-261-4414
           www.maverickhelicopters.com
Las Vegas Helicopters 888-779-0800
           www.lasvegashelicopters.aero
Sundance Helicopters   800-653-1881
           www.sundancehelicopters.com

Best Limo Companies

AWG   702-792-8000
         www.awgcs.com
Bell Trans   702-739-7990
         www.bell-trans.com
CLS Transportation 702-740-4545
         www.lasvegaslimo.com
24-7 Limousines   702-616-0077
         www.24-7limousines.com